World's Fairs

Erik Mattie

World's Fairs

Princeton Architectural Press

Published by
Princeton Architectural Press
37 East Seventh Street
New York City, NY 10003

For a catalog of books published by Princeton
Architectural Press, call toll free 1.800.722.6657 or visit
www.papress.com

Special thanks: Eugenia Bell, Caroline Green,
Clare Jacobson, Therese Kelly, Mark Lamster,
and Annie Nitschke of Princeton Architectural Press—
Kevin C. Lippert, publisher

ISBN 1-56898-132-5

Title page illustration: The Crystal Palace Under Construction

0013988097X

Contents

World's Fairs

TABANGIERS

OISELIERS

LINGERIES

Foreword

The Foire St. Germain
in Paris, covered mar-
kets from 1511

The French national
exhibition of 1834 on
the Place de la
Concorde. Four large
halls astride an axial
boulevard. Such an
arrangement proved
popular for later inter-
national exhibitions

Over the last 150 years, world's fairs have made an important contribution to the history of architecture and design. The prestige associated with such exhibitions combined with their temporary nature have often resulted in spectacular and innovative buildings. Tangible evidence of these structures has, in most cases, disappeared—sometimes accidentally, as in the case of London's Crystal Palace (1851), but more often intentionally, as in the case of Paris's Galerie des Machines (1889). Certain constructions have been preserved and have achieved lasting fame, such as the Eiffel Tower (Paris 1889) and the Unisphere (New York 1964). Le Corbusier's l'Esprit Nouveau Pavilion (Paris 1925) and Ludwig Mies van der Rohe's German Pavilion (Barcelona 1929) have even been reconstructed. But for the many hundreds of pavilions that have failed to withstand the test of time, the enthusiast of the genre is forced to published records. Catalogs, brochures, and other primary source materials dating from the exhibitions sporadically appear on the antiquarian and second-hand market. There are few books on the subject (the most important of these by Wolfgang Friebe and John Allwood, along with a catalog from the Centre Pompidou).[1] Given the lack of availability of these books and taking into account the relevance of the subject, it seemed an excellent idea to the author and publisher to produce a new publication with chronologically arranged visual material. More than three hundred illustrations from thirty world exhibitions provide an initial impression of the richness and diversity of these fantastic events.

1 Friebe's book, Buildings of the World Exhibitions *(Leipzig: Editions Leipzig, 1985) somewhat favors the East and the Gidionesque, while Allwood's book,* The Great Exhibitions *(London: Cassell & Collier Macmillan, 1977) is a broad survey not focusing on architecture. The catalog,* Le livre des expostions universelle: 1851-1989, *from June 1983, takes the same view.*

Introduction

History The first international exhibition, known as the Great Exhibition, was held in Victorian London in 1851. Previous industrial and decorative arts fairs, notably those in England and France, were of a national character. But with the development of industry and the search for new markets the time was ripe for an event on a much larger scale. A precondition for this was the weakening of international trade regulations, which had frustrated commerce in the first half of the nineteenth century.

Since 1851 the idealized view of world trade and world peace marching hand-in-hand has largely remained intact, despite two world wars and countless armed conflicts. The fact that manufacturers of military equipment – notably the German Krupp company – proudly displayed cannons and machine guns at these exhibitions has done little to dispel this optimistic worldview.

World's fairs radiated immense attractiveness. Even with the early exhibitions, when public transportation was still in its infancy, the number of visitors ran into the millions from both those in the host countries and those coming from abroad, including countless dignitaries and royals. For most of these people it was the first opportunity to become acquainted with such new inventions as the elevator, the telephone, and television.

Despite sky-high investment costs and often considerable financial losses, the organization of a world's fair usually meant a step forward for the exhibition host. Export industries thrived, and host cities invested heavily in infrastructure, designing public spaces and accommodations that would, after the event, become permanent. For three cities, a world exhibition was a decisive factor in the decision to build a metro system: Chicago in 1893, Paris in 1900, and Montreal in 1967.

The nature of the world's fairs has changed over time. Since the turn of the century, industry has no longer depended on large international exhibitions. In their place, specialized trade fairs have assumed far greater importance. While the world's fair remains a venue for new products, it is their entertainment value that is now preeminent. Fairgrounds and picturesque historical villages, popular since the last quarter of the nineteenth century, have evolved into the greatest visitor attractions. Participating countries prefer displays that reflect their national identities rather than exhibits of their industrial products. If the original intention was that these events would encourage all countries to live in peace through increased trade, today world peace and free trade have become separate ideals. Nevertheless, world's fairs still constitute a challenge for participating countries to surprise the world with the newest of the new.

Types and organization of fairs There are many different kinds of fairs: international, national, thematic, multilateral, and colonial. In principle, this book reviews only the universal, international exhibitions – those accessible to all countries and for all products – simply because these were the most interesting from an architectural viewpoint. Notable exceptions, however, are the international thematic exhibitions of applied arts held in Turin in 1902 and Paris in 1925. It is only for the largest universal exhibitions that participating nations are expected to design their own pavilions.

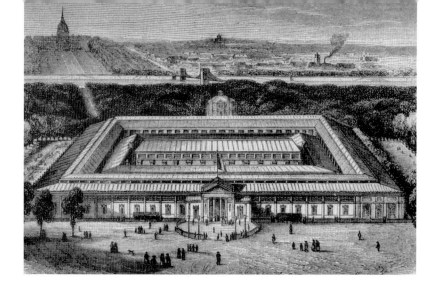

The codes regulating world's fairs were prepared in 1928 and officially set down at a 1931 Paris conference attended by thirty-one nations (not including the United States). In that same year, the supranational organization Bureau International des Expositions (BIE) was founded to establish the dates and locations of future fairs and to broadly oversee their planning and organization, insuring that they meet the organization's rules and requirements. Participating nations are responsible for setting up their own national committees and for the actual organization, financing, and administration of the exhibitions they hold. Before 1931, fairs were organized through the initiative of ambitious heads of state, governments, and influential individuals.

The French national exhibition of 1844 on the Champs Elysées. The prototype for the rectangular exhibition hall surrounded by a classical façade

The architecture of world's fairs
During the nineteenth century, world's fairs presented a powerful stimulus for engineering and construction. The huge halls, which had to accommodate the numerous participants and their displays, demanded new methods of building construction that were not taught at architecture schools like the École des Beaux Arts. New materials like glass, iron, and steel made not only wider spanning possible, but were suitable for building quickly and relatively cheaply. Fair administrators, however, were not always enamored with the idea of revealing the structural components of these miracles of technology, and often disguised glass and steel structures with architecturally designed wood and plasterwork. Indeed, there is a two-sided nature to nineteenth-century world's fairs: daring engineering constructions (for example, the Crystal Palace and the Eiffel Tower) on the one hand, and plastered façades in a predominantly classical style (like those of the World's Columbian Exposition of 1893) on the other. By the turn of the century, especially at the Paris fair of 1900, the architect appeared to have the edge over the engineer, but after World War II there was again much experimentation with new building forms. Glass and steel were celebrated as worthy design elements and there was much experimentation with new construction techniques.

The prototype of the exhibition pavilion is the multinave basilica. This gave rise to a typically elongated form, sometimes with one or more transepts, divided into long galleries punctuated by free-standing columns. The outer walls were either plastered (as at the Paris national exhibition of 1849) or left transparent (as at the Crystal Palace). Deviations from this type appeared but did not enter the pattern book. The basilica prototype became obsolete in the twentieth century, though it did not disappear entirely. An unusual variation was the Symbol Zone at the 1970 Osaka exhibition, where only the rectangular plan recalled the building's illustrious predecessors.

Beyond the communal model of the basilica, world's fairs became spawning grounds for hyperindividual architecture. The Eiffel Tower, the Trylon and Perisphere (New York 1939), and the Atomium (Brussels 1958) remain totally unique. This book celebrates these distinctive buildings as well as their more traditional neighbors.

The Great Exhibition of the Works of Industry of All Nations London

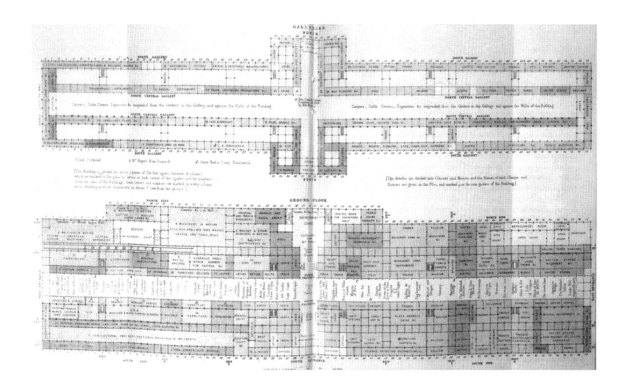

The Crystal Palace after its reconstruction in Sydenham, c. 1855

Plans of the ground floor and galleries

Year **1851 (1 May – 11 October)** Location **London (Hyde Park)** Surface area **26 acres** Visitors **6,039,195** Participating nations **28** Exhibitors **17,062** Architect **Joseph Paxton** Architectural supervisor **Matthew Wyatt** Contractor **Fox Henderson & Co** Novelties **Colt revolvers, false teeth, the telegraph**

It is hard to underestimate the importance of London's Great Exhibition in Hyde Park and the influence of the Crystal Palace on the course of architectural history. While the 1851 exhibition is regarded as the mother of all world's fairs, Sir Joseph Paxton can be seen as the grandfather of modern architecture. The construction of his huge pavilion deviated so far from any previous exhibition building and was so magnificent that it won universal admiration. Queen Victoria and her consort Prince Albert shared with millions of their subjects feelings of extreme pride for this unsurpassed British achievement.

Prolog   The first international world exhibition was born out of the hope that all the peoples of the world might live in harmony, and, more prosaically, out of a desire to tap new potential markets for British products. The fact that only a small and privileged group would initially benefit from the fair was of minor importance. The belief in technology and human ability was immense, and it was envisaged that the selection of goods and affordable products on display from all corners of the world would stimulate trade and industry.

The idea for a world exhibition was suggested by Sir Henry Cole, the assistant keeper of the Public Records Office, who, during his European travels, had visited the large national exhibition of 1849 in Paris. Cole was able to gain Prince Albert's enthusiasm for the project and under royal supervision the British parliament in that same year granted official consent for its organization. A building committee was soon established to be responsible for the construction of an exhibition hall. The committee held a competition among architects and within three weeks no fewer than 245 candidates had responded. The committee gratefully acknowledged the many designs but, after the first round, decided instead to take up Henry Coles' recommendation to employ Joseph Paxton. Paxton had already put himself forward as the man for the job by submitting his plan for an iron and glass construction to the *London News*. It was not a revolutionary concept. In France, Hector Horeau, one of the competition's entrants *nota bene*, was a pioneer in the field of iron and glass construction. Around the time of the competition, similar constructions were being employed for the roofs of two railway stations: London's Kings Cross Station and the Gare de l'Est in Paris. Moreover, this type of structure had been in use for English conservatories for decades.

Paxton, who was a landscape gardener and horticulturist, had built the Great Conservatory at Chatsworth House, Derbyshire (1838–40), and at the time of the competition was engaged in a design for a lily conservatory for the queen. Why not design a similar construction for the exhibition? The ribbed structure of the lily conservatory did in fact serve as a source of inspiration for the construction of the exhibition hall, though Paxton left the technical details to William Henry Barlow, a railway engineer.

Where Paxton's design for an exhibition building differed from those of his predecessors was in its immense proportions. But by using standardized and prefabricated materials, his construction could be built quickly and at relatively low cost. Moreover, there would be no loss of grandeur – a significant consideration due to the royal involvement in the project. The building was certainly majestic: a towering construction with five naves and 1,851 foot sightlines.

Beyond its spectacular and deceptively simple appearance, the Crystal Palace went down in history as a miracle of organization and planning. It's prefabricated materials included no fewer than 3,300 iron stanchions and 300,000 glass plates. The contractors positioned the first stanchion on 26 September 1850 and completed the building just seventeen weeks later. On 1 May 1851 the royal carriages drove out of Buckingham Palace for the opening of an event that may be regarded as the crowning glory of the Industrial Revolution.

Interior
The exceptional dimensions of the building were exaggerated by an additional requirement that a group of monumental elm trees in Hyde Park be preserved. To do this, Paxton spanned the transept with 108-foot vaulting, making its interior as tall as that of Nôtre Dame in Paris. The orientation of the palace was thus determined by four trees. Nearly seventy-five years later, Le Corbusier recalled this environmental gesture by generously saving a tree on the site of his L'esprit Nouveau Pavilion (Paris 1925). Both of these structures had open plans, though with the Crystal Palace it was for practical rather than polemical reasons – it was unclear how the space would be divided among the exhibitors.

A considerable amount of wood was also incorporated into the interior, and the various building parts were painted in primary colors. This innovative color scheme, which provided orientation, was conceived by designer Owen Jones. The floor was also of wood and included parts that had been used as fencing during the building's construction.

13

London 1851

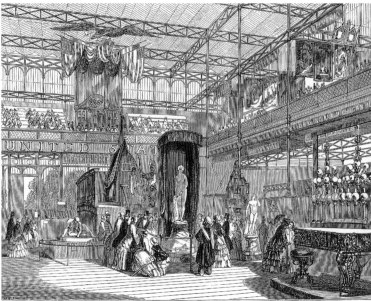

Proposed design by
Hector Horeau for the
exhibition building

The Crystal Palace
under construction

The United States
delegation

A longitudinal view of
Crystal Palace with the
southern main entrance
and barrel vaulting

Exhibition building during construction

Competition-winning design

Paxton's design, before addition of transept

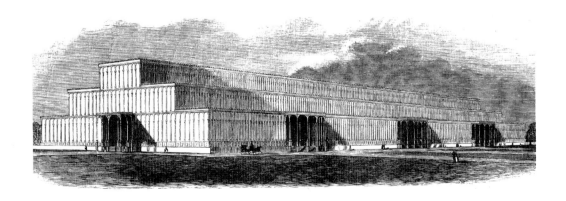

Bird's-eye perspective
of the Crystal Palace
and Hyde Park

The northern entrance
to the transept of the
Crystal Palace

The hoisting of the bar-
rel vaulting, which was
assembled on the
ground

Model of a worker's
dwelling designed by
Henry Roberts at Prince
Albert's request

The exhibition The desire to participate in the exhibition was so great that even if only the British entries
were to be accommodated the space would have been too small. It was left to the foreign countries to select their own
entries, provided they did not overstep their designated few square feet of space. In England, several committees were
set up to determine who would and would not be allotted room. Prince Albert had originally suggested classifying
entries as raw materials, general products, or decorative elements but this proved too broad-based. In the end, there
were four main groups: raw materials, machines, manufactured products, and applied arts and these were then subdivided into thirty additional categories. Fine arts were not represented as the exhibition was of an industrial nature. The
judging was based on a French system, and Henry Cole was responsible for its administration. At the opening, only one-
tenth of the foreign sections were unoccupied. The house rules were strict but fair: no alcohol, smoking, or dogs – the
latter to the dismay of every true Englishman

Profit The £186,000 profit from the exhibition was earmarked for educational purposes. Land was purchased in
South Kensington with the aim of creating an area devoted to art and technology. In this space the Science and
Geological museums, the Imperial College of Science and Technology, and the Royal Colleges of Art and Music were
later built – in addition, of course, to Royal Albert Hall and the Victoria and Albert Museum.

Epilog The Crystal Palace, as it was dubbed by *Punch* magazine, was much imitated in Europe and the United
States. Similar structures arose at fairs in Dublin, New York, Munich, and Amsterdam. More significant, however, is the
fact that reproductions of the London prototype hung in the homes of people in the most remote corners of the world.
The nineteenth-century had taken modern architecture to heart.

Originally intended as a temporary structure, the Crystal Palace was painstakingly dismantled in 1854 and rebuilt in
Sydenham, south of London, as a permanent exhibition pavilion. In 1936 the great building went up in flames.

Exposition Universelle Paris

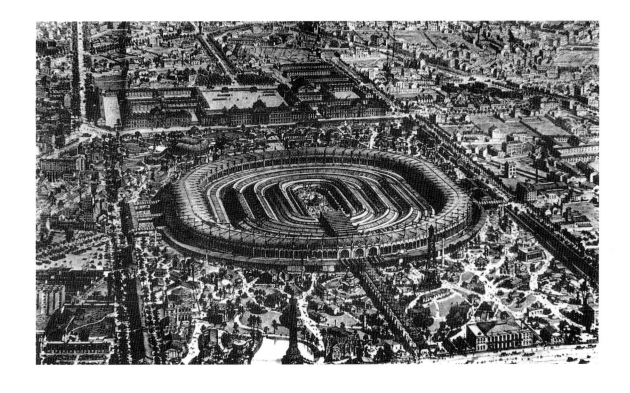

Plan of the exhibition
site with Main Building
and smaller pavilions

Bird's-eye view of the
exhibition site

Year **1867 (1 April – 31 October)** Location **Paris (Champ de Mars)** Surface area **165 acres** Attendance **6.8 million** Participating nations **32** Exhibitors **60,000** Engineer **Jean-Baptiste Krantz** Commissaire Général **Frédéric Le Play** Novelties **Artificial limbs, the hydraulic elevator, reinforced concrete, the rocking chair**

Between London and Paris After London, exhibitions followed in Paris (1855) and again in London (1862) that were similar in concept and size, but architecturally uninventive. Smaller exhibitions were also held in Dublin and New York. The buildings for these exhibitions were based, like the Crystal Palace, on a rectangle subdivided into elongated halls. But where the Crystal Palace had delighted the world with its daring, open design and its clearly visible system of construction, its successors fell back on the architectural styles of past generations. New, however, was that in 1855 the fine arts were admitted as a separate category and were even allocated their own building. Machinery was also given a separate facility.

Engineer and architect The contrast between functionalist buildings – like the London Crystal Palace – and some of the more traditionally designed pavilions that followed it is partly the result of shifting balances of power between architects and engineers. More technically oriented engineers were generally responsible for construction. Then there were the architects, who designed according to the rules of classical composition as taught at the École des Beaux Arts. In fact it was not unusual for engineers and architects to collaborate at an exhibition, sometimes even on one building. For this reason, following the London exhibition a prototype was developed using a plastered façade with an inner core of glass and steel. These were generally rectangular buildings animated by corner and central pavilions. Not all exhibition buildings, however, conformed to this type, as demonstrated at the 1867 Paris fair.

Main building The location for the 1867 exhibition was not the Champs Elysées, as it was in 1855, but the much larger Champ de Mars, which had been used for the French national exhibition of 1798. The Main Building was oval with seven concentrically arranged halls, each housing a particular type of product. The advantage of this design, conceived (but not executed) by George Maw and Edward Payne for the 1862 London exhibition, was that segments of the building could be divided up among participating countries like slices of a cake. In this way, the visitor could choose between a comparative study of a specific category of product (by circling the building) or take in what one particular country had to offer (by moving in and out). In practice, the classification model did not work particularly well, as not every country could display a sufficient number of products in each category.

Previous exhibitions had shown that products on floors above ground level drew less attention than those on the first floor. It was thus decided to hold the whole event on one level. This required a massive surface area: 1,281 × 1,608 feet. A central avenue – with installations on the theme "History of the Earth" – divided the building along its central, longitudinal axis, and this was intersected at its midpoint, in the building's center, by a second main thoroughfare. An open courtyard occupied the central space, planted with palm trees and adorned with sculptures.

The building took optimal advantage of the elongated form of the Champ de Mars. The proposal for the oval exhibition building (the first in that shape) came from the Commissaire Général, the well-known engineer and social economist Frédéric le Play, who was also responsible for the 1855 Paris exhibition. He developed the concept in close collaboration with the nephew of Emperor Napoleon III, Prince Napoleon, who had also held a position of authority in 1855.

The Paris Exhibition Building of 1855

The Main Building under construction

Cross-section of the Galerie des Machines

Cross-section of the central gallery

Elevation and cross-section of the Main Building

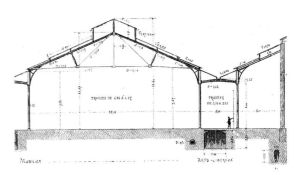

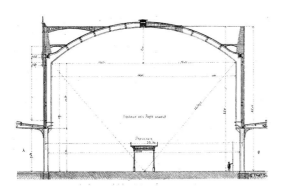

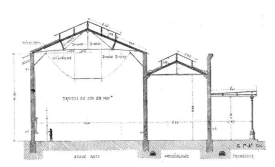

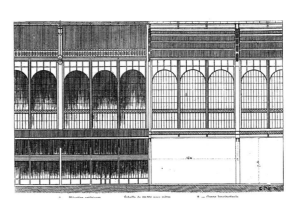

View of galleries in the
Main Building

Restaurant and pro-
menade along the
exterior of the Main
Building

The hydraulic elevator, a novelty that took visitors to the roof of the Main Building

Exhibited decorative pottery elements from the Muller Company

Exhibited hollow bricks for the dividing wall of a wine cellar

Construction details with, upper left, the Galerie des Machines

Elevation and plan of a model dwelling (the iron frame supports walls made from hollow bricks), architect M. S. Ferrand

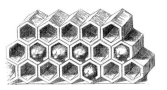

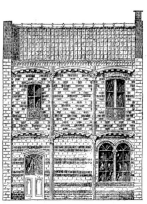

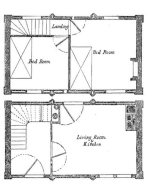

Galerie des Machines

The outer circular hall of the Main Building, the Galerie des Machines, was a raised area with a view across the building interior toward the central courtyard. Eighty-five feet high and 115 feet across, the Galerie des Machines was a *tour de force* of engineering. Encircling the gallery at a lower level were cafés and restaurants constructed entirely from iron and glass. These opened to the exterior of the building in the evenings, providing a splendid promenade lit by gas lamps and covered by an awning. The clerestory of the Galerie des Machines, which protruded above the circle of restaurants, was designed with tall windows and a rather plain balustrade that became somewhat more decorative above the entrances. The appearance of the Main Building was thus in keeping with the new engineering/construction trend set by the Crystal Palace, and not in the Beaux-Arts tradition, like the exhibition halls of 1855 and 1862.

Idealism and commercialism

The designer of the Main Building was Jean-Baptiste Krantz, an engineer of bridges and roads, assisted by the architects Léopold Hardy, Charles Duval, and a young engineer named Gustave Eiffel. It was Le Play, however, who suggested the oval plan. His reasoning was not practical but symbolic: two half circles would represent the northern and southern hemispheres. It was also Le Play who introduced the idea of a thematic installation within the building, "The History of Labor." This was placed around the central courtyard along the "Colisée du Travail." Thus the Paris fair had an idealistic agenda in addition to its more prosaic commercial goals.

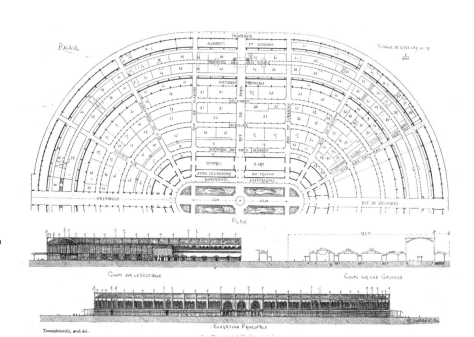

Partial plan of the Main Building with cross-section and elevations

View from the roof walkway accessed via hydraulic elevator

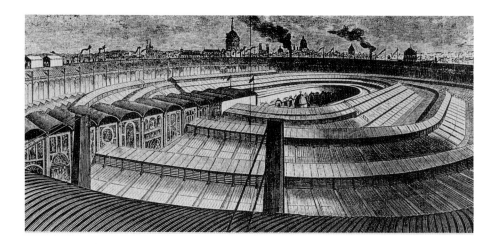

**Exterior view of the
Main Building from
across the Seine**

The site Beyond its classification system, the 1867 Paris exhibition was innovative in many other respects. It was the first fair, for example, to remain open in the evenings. It was also the first time that an exhibition included thematic pavilions in addition to a main building; the grounds surrounding the Main Building were a veritable amusement park. Diverse and exotic in style, theme pavilions became a hallmark of later fairs. The 1867 site, designed by Le Play, boasted a "housing" section with full-scale architectural models, including a house for middle-class workers designed by M. S. Ferrand. The detailing was carefully executed and the rooms were spacious. There were also houses exhibiting various regional styles – a Swiss châlet, for example – forerunners of the picturesque villages at later fairs, as well as such divergent structures as a lighthouse, an Indian temple, a Tunisian coffee house, and a stable for camels. The only building that has withstood the test of time is the Bardo, the small palace of the Bey of Tunis that was rebuilt in the Parc de Montsouris.

Weltausstellung Vienna

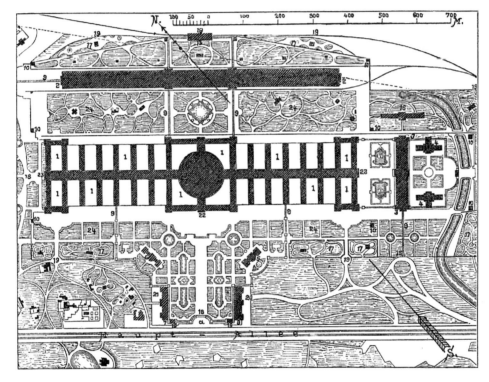

Fig. 1123. Situation der Wiener Weltausstellung im Jahre 1873.

1) Industriepalast. 2) Maschinenhalle. 3) Kunsthalle. 4) Exposition des Amateurs. 5) Kaiser-Pavillon. 6) Pavillon der Jury. 7) Verwaltungs-Bureau. 8) Post und Telegraph. 9) Verbindungs-Gallerien. 10) Wachthäuser.
13) Eisenbahnstation. a—18) Haupteingänge. 19) Nebeneingänge. 20) Weg zum Kaiser-Pavillon. 21) Weg nach dem Pavillon der Jury. 22) Haupteingang des Industriepalastes. 23) Nebeneingang desselben. 24) Plätze für Pavillons.

The Rotunda

Plan of the site with the skeletal form of the Main Building clearly visible

Year **1873 (1 May — 1 November)** Location **Vienna (the Prater)** Surface area **42 acres** Visitors **7 million (53,000 stands)** General Manager **Dr. Wilhelm von Schwarz-Sendborn**

Austria was conferred with the honor of being the first German-speaking nation to host a universal exhibition. It would also be the last German-language fair for a long time. Notwithstanding future events, in 1873 Vienna was rapidly becoming the foremost metropolis of central Europe. The Wiener Ringstrasse was under construction and a glorious future appeared to lie ahead for the capital of the Austro-Hungarian Empire. An international exhibition was judged an eminently suitable means of making other nations aware of this. But the event was to end gravely: the Viennese stock market collapsed and Europe found itself in the midst of financial calamity; visitors feared an outbreak of cholera and were otherwise deterred by the high prices for accommodation; it rained incessantly throughout the fair; and, to cap matters off, the roof of the main exhibition building leaked.

Site and Main Building The exhibition site was the Prater, a former royal hunting refuge along the Danube that had been transformed into a city park. In fact, the Danube was redirected by nearly half a mile to help create the site. The Main Building, like the exhibition halls of 1855 (Paris) and 1862 (London), was built in a pompous neo-Renaissance style, but distinguished itself with an exceptional plan, a plan that can be viewed as the summation of all previous fair halls. While the building was in the standard rectangular shape, it was sectioned off by seventeen transept halls. There was, however, only one 3,000 foot central corridor bisecting the transepts. The original idea for this structure came from Eduard van der Nüll and August von Siccardsburg, well-known for the Neue Hofoper on the Ringstrasse. The three central transepts were linked via corridors on their outer edges and bordered the Rotunda, a giant domed structure. Austrian confidence was not such, however, that the hosts dared to build the Main Building themselves. For this they commissioned Englishman John Scott Russell. The wrought-iron and glass dome of the Rotunda was supported by thirty-two 79-foot pillars and had a ribbed supporting structure partly visible from the exterior but hidden by excessive ornament on the interior. The diameter of the lantern was approximately 100 feet; that of the whole dome 351 feet. The observatory platform was 100 feet above ground; the lantern, with its huge crown, was 279 feet high. Intended for use as a corn exchange after the exhibition, the Rotunda was the largest structure ever built without interposed buttresses.

Peasant house from the
Alsace region. Instead
of the workers' housing
displayed at fairs in
industrialized France
and England, the
Vienna exhibition pre-
sented an international
collection of peasant
farmhouses

Southern and eastern
entrances to the Main
Building (above) and
two entrances to the
site in the form of tri-
umphal arches (below)

Karl von Hasenauer was responsible for the neo-Renaissance ornamentation of both the halls and the Rotunda. He later did much work on the Ringstrasse in a style influenced by Gottfried Semper and his teachers Van der Nüll and Siccardsburg. The Rotunda was actually the only building that was open at the beginning of the exhibition. The rest followed during the second half of June.

Other buildings
The Palace of Industry was similar in concept to the Machinery Hall of the 1855 Paris fair, though the latter, at nearly 4,000 feet, was one-and-a-half times as long. Like the Rotunda, the Palace of Industry was not seen as a temporary building – after the exhibition it was to be converted into a grain storage facility.

The Paris-initiated tradition of international pavilions continued at Vienna; official presentations of products were housed in the Main Building; various regional buildings were reproduced as full-scale models in a romantic village setting. Since Austria was still predominantly agrarian, peasant homes from all over the world were exhibited (at French and English fairs, workers' housing was presented). And for the first time agriculture had its own building, the start of a tradition that continues to this day.

29

Bird's-eye perspective
of the exhibition site.
Painting by Johann
Lange, Museum der
Stadt, Wien

Interior view of the
Rotunda

The fair's Entrance Hall, which has often been derided as architectural kitsch, was exuberant, hierarchical, and imposingly designed. But even if flamboyant, it recalled the classically-based, triumphal-arch style employed at the Main Building of the 1855 Paris fair. The Vienna exhibition, despite the spectacular Rotunda, was thus in keeping with a more restrained Beaux-Arts design tradition.

A special transportation system was developed for the event; various train tracks ran to the site, and on the perimeter there was parking for carriages. Plagued as it was, however, the fair often remained empty, incurring heavy financial losses in the process. Despite the best intentions of preservationists, there remains no tangible evidence of the Weltausstellung aside from a Ferris wheel in the Prater.

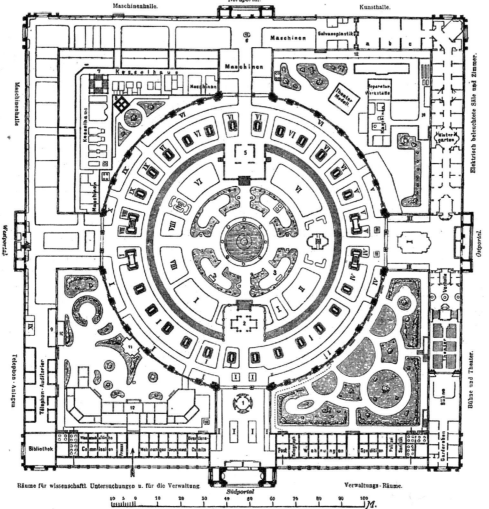

Plan of the Rotunda

Fig. 1124. Plan der Rotunde der Wiener Weltausstellung, für die internat. elektrische Ausstellung 1883 eingerichtet.

I) Oesterreich-Ungarn. II) Belgien. III) England. IV) Italien. V) Dänemark. VI) Frankreich. VII) Türkei. VIII) Deutschland. IX) Russland. X) Schweiz. XI) Amerika. — 1) Kaiserpavillon. 2) K. k. österr. Handelsministerium. 3) Buffets. 4) Fontäne. 5) Franz. Ministerium. 6) Leuchtthurm. 7) Bremsthurm. 8) Schornstein. 9) Dunkelkammer. 10) Accumulatoren. 11) Musikpavillon. 12) Restauration.

Centennial Exposition Philadelphia

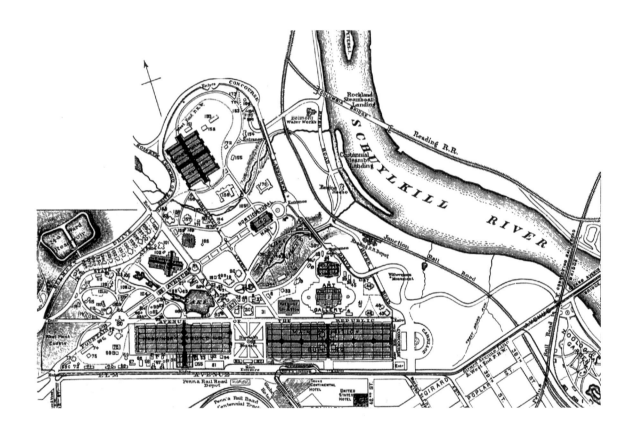

Interior of the Main
Building

Plan of the exhibition
site

Year **1876 (10 May – 10 November)** Location
Philadelphia (Fairmount Park) Surface area **284.5
acres** Attendance **9,910,966** Exhibitors **14,420** Chief
architect **Herman Joseph Schwarzmann** Novelties
**The Declaration of Independence, the sewing
machine, the telephone, the typewriter**

The United States, impressed by the 1851 London exhibition, held its first world's fair two years later in New York. The form of that exhibition hall, though not its scale, followed the example of the Crystal Palace. Internal discord and an aloof government, resulted in an unsuccessful event. The burden of rectifying this blot on the American record fell to Philadelphia, which would host a fair to surpass all previous ones. The exhibition celebrated the centennial of American independence, proclaimed one hundred years earlier in Philadelphia.

For a young nation of boundless opportunity and energy, the production of a large exhibition presented little problem. Unlike earlier European fairs, which courted foreign markets, the Philadelphia exhibition needed only to focus on the homefront. Fast-growing American industry was barely able to meet ever-increasing internal demand. Moreover, the United States was heavily protected from foreign goods by all manner of import restrictions. These restrictions, along with the attendant high costs for such distant travel, discouraged many European nations – with the important exception of France – from participating. When it closed, the fair's financial losses – offset by government subsidy – would be great.

The site   Visitors to the exhibition – both American and foreign – were impressed with the host country's technological leaps forward, by the huge pavilions, and by the immensity of the site, which was one-and-a-half times bigger than that of the largest previous exhibition (Paris 1867). Space was required for 250 small and large buildings. Design on such a large scale required careful planning, both logistically and artistically, as well as a coherent urban vision.

The chosen site was the uneven terrain of Fairmount Park, which lay adjacent to the Schuylkill River. A young but experienced landscape architect, Herman Joseph Schwarzmann, was responsible for preparing the park for the exhibition, which he did in record time. His design included landscaped elements in which water – in the form of a lake and meandering streams – played a major aesthetic role. The pavilions were scattered as separate entities throughout the landscape. A more formal design enclosed the main pavilions within a network of linear streets. To the sides of the Main Entrance were Machinery Hall and the Main Building, separated by a geometrically designed courtyard. From the square, a diagonal avenue ran at right angles to the other main axis of the exhibition, Fountain Avenue. In turn, this avenue led straight to another important structure, the Horticultural Building. The axes intersected at the center of the site. A railway brought visitors to the park, and an elevated railway – a prototype of the monorail systems that would appear at later fairs – transported them about the fairgrounds. The site itself was bounded by new hotels built to cater to the expected flood of visitors.

Main building The Main Building, constructed of iron, glass, tile, and steel sheeting (a new material rapidly replacing cast iron) measured 1,892 x 561 feet and was thus the largest exhibition building yet constructed. It was of the rectangular, three-nave type familiar to exhibition structures, with corner and central pavilions. In a vaguely classical style, the façade concealed the building's construction system, though the steel-sheeting of the roof was clearly visible from the inside. The ornament of the interior iron sections was traditional, while the exterior was more restrained and more American. The Main Building was originally the subject of a competition but, as with the 1851 London exhibition, in the end the participants were thanked and Schwarzmann's design for a larger pavilion was accepted. From the competition entries, those of Calvert Vaux & George K. Radford and Henry A. & James P. Sims were chosen as guidelines. Engineer Henry Pettit and his associate Joseph Wilson, who had not taken part in the competition, were then asked to distill a new design from these ideas. Towers – seen as too costly and unnecessary – were expressly omitted from the design brief, but were later included to give the building a more decorative look. Four years after the exhibition closed, the building was demolished.

The Globe Hotel, one of
several new hotels built
on the periphery of the
exhibition site

Plan of the Main
Building

Memorial Hall art
gallery

The Agricultural
Building

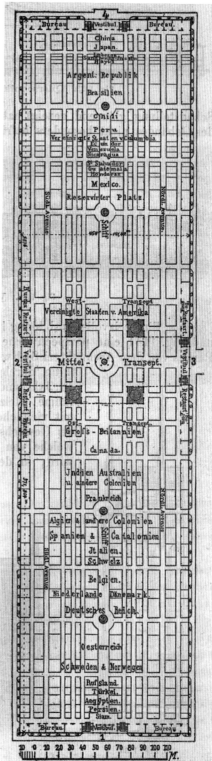

Fig. 1132. Grundriss vom Hauptgebäude.
1) Oestlicher Eingang, 2) südlicher Eingang,
3) zur Kunsthalle, 4) zur Maschinenhalle.

MEMORIAL BUILDING OR ART GALLERY—INTERNATIONAL EXHIBITION.

365 feet in length and 210 feet in width.

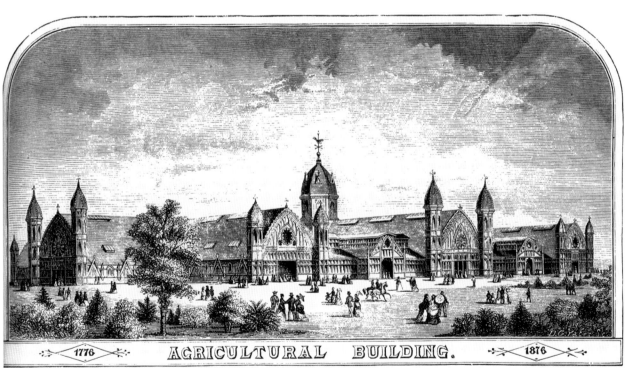

1776   AGRICULTURAL BUILDING.   1876

AGRICULTURAL HALL—INTERNATIONAL EXHIBITION.

820 feet in length and 540 feet in width.

Other buildings The fair's other large pavilions had also been typologically proven, though their forms were, to some extent, original. The Art Gallery, intended as a permanent addition to the city and designed by Schwarzmann, was based on the classical teachings of the École des Beaux Arts. Schwarzmann also designed the Horticultural Building and a few smaller buildings. The Women's Pavilion, a domed Greek cross constructed in an eclectic style, was financed by women and filled with work created by female artists and craftsmen (the Women's Committee also commissioned a march from Richard Wagner for the occasion). The exhibition's second largest building was Machinery Hall, which was similar in appearance to the Main Building. This is not surprising, as its designers were the engineers Pettit and Wilson, who were also responsible for several bridges on the site. For the first time, guest nations were allocated separate pavilions in order to present their own products. The Horticultural Building, in Moorish-eclectic style, was intended as a permanent structure and survived until 1955, when it burned. In addition to the Art Gallery, which lives on under the name Memorial Hall (North Concourse), the Ohio State Building also escaped demolition.

One of the biggest attractions at the exhibition was the giant hand and torch of the Statue of Liberty, then still under construction. The Declaration of Independence, on loan from Washington, also drew many of visitors. Barely a decade after the final shots of the Civil War, the Centennial Exposition celebrated the union that had nearly dissolved and the freedoms that union guaranteed.

HORTICULTURAL HALL—INTERNATIONAL EXHIBITION.
383 feet in length and 193 feet in width.

The Horticultural
Building

The modest Main
Entrance to the site

The Photographic
Art Gallery

Machinery Hall

Bird's-eye view of the exhibition site

The hand and torch of the Statue of Liberty

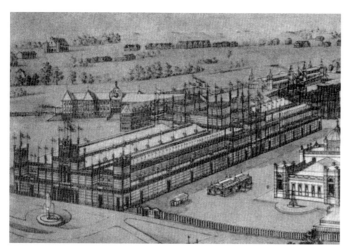

The octagonal Arkansas
Pavilion

The Spanish Pavilion

Exposition Universelle Paris

Year **1878 (1 May – 31 October)** Location **Paris (Champ de Mars, Trocadéro)** Surface area **192 acres** Attendance **16 million** Commissaire Général **Jean-Baptiste Krantz** Architect **Léopold Hardy** Novelties **The ice machine, electric lighting**

Interior of the Palais
de l'Industrie during an
awards ceremony

Bird's-eye view of the
exhibition site

Despite the fact that France, like the rest of Europe in the 1870s, was financially pressed, President Marie Macmahon nevertheless announced on 4 April 1876 that Paris would once again host an international exhibition. No doubt he wanted to prove that despite its defeat in the Franco-Prussian War, the vicissitudes of the Paris Commune, and its deplorable economic situation France was still an important power. As the date set for the exhibition was barely two years after Macmahon's decree, it is small wonder that at the opening ceremonies much of the fair was still under scaffolding – a problem typical at future exhibitions.

Repetition   The 1878 exhibition was a repeat of the Paris 1867 exhibition, both in a material sense and in regard to the people involved. Engineer Jean-Baptiste Krantz, chief designer in 1867, succeeded Le Play as the Commissaire Général. Gustave Eiffel, Charles Duval, and Léopold Hardy were also reinlisted for the 1878 event. As in 1867, the Main Building was arranged according to the different categories of products on display, though its overall shape was rectangular, not oval. The pavilions of foreign nations were restricted to a central promenade, the "Rue des Nations," where their divergent façades made for a flamboyant patchwork. A permanent conference hall was built next to the temporary Main Building.

The Statue of Liberty, last seen in Philadelphia, also reappeared in Paris. This time, the head of Frédéric-Auguste Bartholdi's colossus was exhibited in a vestibule of the Palais de l'Industrie.

Site   On the suggestion of Eugène Emmanuel Viollet-le-Duc, the *eminence grise* of French architecture and engineering, it was decided to once again hold the exhibition on the Champ de Mars. This time, however, the exhibition would also make use of a site on the opposite bank of the Seine, the Trocadéro. A competition was held for both sites: a temporary exhibition hall of the usual immense dimensions was planned for the Mars field, a smaller though just as grand conference building was envisaged for the other side. From the ninety-four entries, the jury chose the engineers Jules Desiré Bourdais and Gabriel J. A. Davioud to design the Trocadéro and Hardy to execute the main exhibition building, the Palais de l'Industrie. The central axis of the latter building ran in a straight line, via the specially extended Pont d'Iéna, to the fountains in the center of the Trocadéro. Around the large buildings were smaller structures set in a landscaped park, although there were not as many as at the 1867 fair.

The Moorish village in Torcadéro park

Rear of the Trocadéro, engineer J. D. Bourdais and architect Gabriel J. A. Davioud

The Trocadéro under construction

Palais de l'Industrie Measuring 1,135 x 2,312 feet, the immense hall easily outstripped in size its Philadelphia rival of 1876. In actual floor area the difference was even greater, as the Paris building also boasted a basement level. There were two reasons for the basement: it made a level floor possible across the highly uneven surface of the Champ de Mars, and the space underneath could be used for an ingenious network of ventilation pipes. This system, which made Paris 1878 the first climate-controlled exhibition, ensured that even on hot summer days the temperature inside would remain comfortable. In cross-section, the Palais was similar to the Main Building of 1867: a series of interconnecting galleries. A rectangular layout was chosen so that when the exhibition was dismantled, the standardized building elements would be easier to reuse. As in the earlier fair, a wider, taller, and elevated Machinery Hall was located along the outer edge. The roof of this section required a dynamic construction system that was more complex than that for the rest of the building. Consisting of a Tudor-style half-timbered framework, the Galerie des Machines was 82 feet high and 115 feet wide – with no intermediate columns or supports (weight was distributed to the foundations through

Each of the invited
nations built its own
façade along the Rue
des Nations

The Paris Pavilion, architect Joseph Bouvard

The completed
Trocadéro

The Swedish Tower in
Trocadéro park

The Russian façade on
the Rue des Nations

the building's framework). The daring construction was conceived by Henri de Dion, an engineer appointed by Krantz. Alas, de Dion never saw his brainchild realized; he died before the building was completed. The glass exterior wall was illuminated from the interior by electric lights, direct forerunners of Edison's light bulbs. Gustave Eiffel was responsible for constructing the curved metal roofs of the pavilions and for a vestibule on the north side. Stylistically, these halls exhibited the principles of the École des Beaux Arts, though the use of glass and iron lent them an unconventional, modern air. The master plan of the Palais de l'Industrie was by Léopold Hardy, assisted by Charles Duval. An internal transport system, hidden under the floor sections, made it easier to assemble and dismantle the building. With the Palais de l'Industrie, Paris demonstrated that it held a place all its own in the history of exhibition architecture.

Instead of the proven basilica model, an attempt was once again made to create a building that was not only architecturally interesting but functionally conceived.

Other buildings The Trocadéro was modeled on a Roman amphitheater: a neo-Roman construction beneath a nineteenth-century dome. Two Moorish minarets stood over its neobaroque wings. The building, for all its eclecticism, was still regarded as modern. The contrast between the highly decorative Trocadéro and the highly functional Palais de l'Industrie was intentional; the former was also designed for conferences and concerts and was planned to be used for years to come. Special features included four thousand electric lamps, a hydraulic elevator, and an air-conditioning system. From the Moorish towers there was a splendid view over the exhibition site. The Trocadéro was demolished to make way for the 1937 world exhibition and replaced by another pavilion, also intended for permanent use. In the park surrounding the Trocadéro were various attractions and a small number of pavilions, including one for an ice machine.

The Galerie des Machines, seen from the British section

The American façade on
the Rue des Nations

The Japanese and
Chinese façades on the
Rue des Nations

The Main Building
under construction

Widening of the Pont
d'Iéna

The Main Building from
the Quai d'Orsay

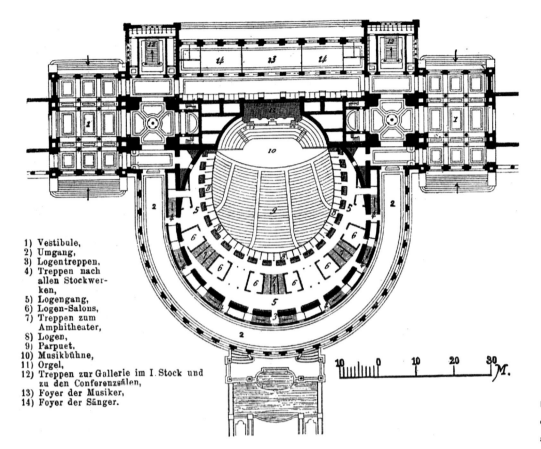

1) Vestibule,
2) Umgang,
3) Logentreppen,
4) Treppen nach allen Stockwerken,
5) Logengang,
6) Logen-Salons,
7) Treppen zum Amphitheater,
8) Logen,
9) Parpuet,
10) Musikbühne,
11) Orgel,
12) Treppen zur Gallerie im I. Stock und zu den Conferenzsälen,
13) Foyer der Musiker,
14) Foyer der Sänger.

Map of the Trocadéro,
engineer J. D. Bourdais
and architect Gabriel
J. A. Davioud

The Spanish façade on
the Rue des Nations

Sydney International Exhibition Sydney
International Exhibition Melbourne

Year **1879–80 (17 October – 20 April)** Location **Sydney**
Surface area **15 acres** Attendance **1,117,536** Chief Architect
James Barnet Novelty **Passenger Elevator**

**The German section of
the Garden Palace,
Sydney**

**Garden Palace, from
Sydney harbor, architect
James Barnet**

Year **1880–81 (October – May)** Location **Melbourne**
Surface area **63 acres** Attendance **1,330,297** Participating
nations **37** Chief architect **Reed & Barnes**

The 1879–80 universal exhibition in Sydney, held just before that of its Melbourne rival, was the first in a series of fairs on the Australian continent. After Melbourne came Adelaide (1887), then Melbourne again (1888–89), followed by Brisbane (1897), Hobart (1894), and then, nearly a century later, Brisbane for a second time (1988).Brisbane expects to play host for a third time in 2002. The number of visitors to both the Sydney and Melbourne fairs was significantly higher than expected considering the accessibility of Australia and the fact that the Paris fair had been held so recently. The number of participating countries was also surprisingly high – Britain, Japan, the United States, and most nations from the European continent were represented.

Within a relatively short period, Australia had developed from an inhospitable penal colony into a civilized, democratic nation. In 1879 the idea for an international exhibition in the city of Melbourne, Victoria, was proposed and an official request was submitted to Parliament. Slighted, the older city of Sydney in the gold-rich province of New South Wales decided to organize an exhibition of its own. It was carried through with such gusto that Sydney caught up with Melbourne during their concurrent preparations.

The Sydney and Melbourne fairs commenced a decade in which many large and small exhibitions were held around the world, often with more than one opening in a given year. In general, these were not outstanding events with daring architectural constructions; rather, they were aimed at augmenting and protecting commercial interests. In this vein, the goal of the Australian exhibitions was to focus the eyes of the world, in particular those of their international trading partners, on Australia. In this light, the increased exposure and invigorated trade created by the Sydney and Melbourne fairs made them successful.

The great fire of 22
September 1882 com-
pletely destroyed the
Garden Palace, Sydney.
Watercolor by John
Clark Hoyte, Mitchell
Library, State Library of
New South Wales

Garden Palace, Sydney,
from park side

Melbourne, Main
Building

Sydney The site chosen for the Sydney exhibition was a landscaped area close to the city's harbor now occupied by the Royal Botanical Gardens. After some initial public protest against the destruction of the city's skyline within view of the open harbor, work was begun on the main pavilion, the Garden Palace.

The Garden Palace elaborated on the nineteenth-century tradition of ingenious iron and glass structures wrapped in pretentious, classical packaging. The building's architect was James Barnet, also known for Sydney's Customs House and Lands Department Building. The floor plan took the form of a Greek cross and measured 800 feet at its two longest points. A 210 foot dome with a diameter of roughly 100 feet was placed at the crossing. Square towers with open lanterns punctuated the composition. The dome, towers, and foundation were mainly in stone, while the rest of the building was constructed of glass, corrugated iron, and wood. The latter material was undoubtedly to blame for the Garden Palace going tragically and irretrievably up in flames on 22 September 1882 after having done long service as the city's Mining and Technological Museum. From an architectural standpoint the building was not innovative, but because the desire to surpass Melbourne demanded an intense building tempo, Sydney did achieve an interesting first in the building trade: artificially lit with electric light, construction work went on throughout the night.

Contemporary photograph of the Melbourne Main Building, architects Reed & Barnes

Interior of the Sydney Garden Palace dome

Melbourne The province of Victoria, like New South Wales, possessed rich veins of gold that had greatly contributed to the nation's prosperity. The capital of Victoria was Melbourne, a city that in the brief history of its existence already had ample experience in organizing national and colonial exhibitions. The fact that Sydney took precedence in holding the first world's fair on Australian soil was a bitter pill, but it did not prevent Melbourne from opening a second fair in the year that Sydney's exhibition closed. One benefit of this was that international exhibitors were not forced to make two trips to Australia, but could move on to the new location with ease. The Main Building, situated on an unattractive and bleak plain that had been transformed for the occasion into what is now known as Carlton Gardens, adjoined a covered courtyard with two temporary wooden wings at each end. The central pavilion of the still extant Main Building lay on the axis of the courtyard. The architects were Reed & Barnes, the former (Joseph Reed), one of Australia's foremost nineteenth-century architects, a builder who left a particularly strong mark on the city of Melbourne. Between 1888 and 1889 the Main Building was enlarged to accommodate a second fair, the Centennial International Exhibition, which marked the discovery of the continent. The plan of the building was on the basilica model, and the pomp and circumstance of its neo-Renaissance architecture gave the desired impression that Australia was keeping up with the rest of the world.

Neither the Sydney nor the Melbourne fair featured any groundbreaking inventions. Whereas Sydney was more an agricultural exhibition, Melbourne – in the tradition of the great fairs – emphasized industrial products. Sydney did, however, feature the first passenger elevator on Australian soil. The elevator was an apt metaphor for the two exhibitions, which Australia used to propel itself into the lofty status of the great powers.

Internationale Koloniale en Uitvoerhandelstentoonstelling Amsterdam

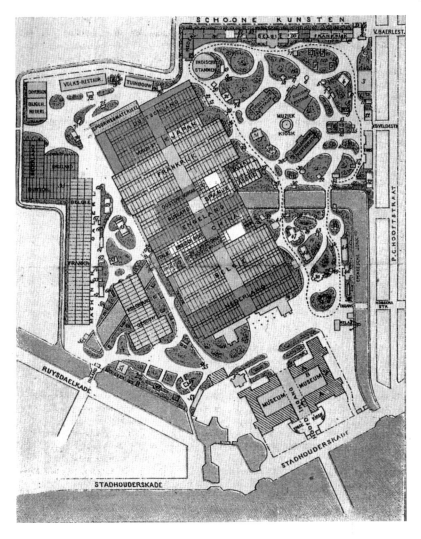

The Rijksmuseum, which served as the main entrance to the exhibition

Map of the exhibition with, lower right, the still unfinished Rijksmuseum

Year **1883 (1 May – 31 October)** Location **Amsterdam (the Museumplein)** Surface area **54.3 acres** Attendance **1.4 million** Participating countries **28** Commissioner **Edouard Agostini** Developer **Tasson and Washer** Novelty **Colonial village with indigenous peoples**

Bird's-eye view of the exhibition site with the Main Building at left, the Royal Pavilion at lower right, and just above it, the well-attended international restaurants. Drawing by Johan Conrad Greive Jr.

In the second half of the nineteenth century the Netherlands looked to take its place as an equal among the great nations, and Amsterdam, under the inspired leadership of businessmen like Dr. Samuel Sarphatie, sought the cosmopolitan flavor of cities like London and Paris. What better to assert the city's expanding role than a world's fair. Many average Amsterdammers, however, did not agree that holding the first world exhibition on Dutch soil was such a good idea. They argued that it would attract relatively few visitors and that a lack of monumental architecture and a modest exhibition site would mean an event with the dimensions of a village fair. Criticism was also leveled at the many foreigners involved in the planning, financing, and construction of the exhibition, criticism that, given the international flavor of the event, was strange to say the least.

An international exhibition
In 1880 a young and unknown businessman, Edouard Agostini, suggested the city host an international exhibition. After some initial skepticism, prominent Amsterdammers came to Agostini's support. But the Dutch government refused to pledge any money for the event up-front, forcing Agostini, who was charged with the day-to-day operations of a specially created exhibition committee, to search for foreign investors. Through contacts in France and Belgium, Agostini eventually found a little-known Belgian firm, Tasson and Washer, that was prepared to build the Main Building in exchange for all of the entrance fees and the proceeds from leasing exhibition space. Agostini agreed. These concessions, combined with the fact that mainly French and Belgian architects and laborers were responsible for the fair's construction, created suspicion and resentment among the local population. Fears were realized when Tasson and Washer went bankrupt despite the exhibition's high returns, and independent investors received a return of only one fifth of their investments.

Notwithstanding these vicissitudes and the modest site, the Amsterdam exhibition, the first with a colonial theme, made several noteworthy contributions to the history of world's fairs. Not only were entire dwellings from overseas colonies erected, but these structures were actually inhabited – during the day at least – by indigenous peoples. After Amsterdam 1883 native villages, living anthropological exhibits complete with "savages," became fixtures at world's fairs, ostensibly demonstrating the progress and superiority of Western culture while allowing fairgoers the *frisson* of an encounter with the exotic. Amsterdam 1883 was also unique in that its emphasis lay more on the trade of industrial products rather than their manufacture – a typically Dutch spin.

The entrance to the
Main Building during
the official opening.
The proportions in the
drawing are not accu-
rate

Façade of the Main
Building with canvas
"shawl."

The site

Amsterdam's existing exhibition building, the Crystal Palace-inspired Paleis voor Volksvlijt, was not nearly as large as its London predecessor, and could not accommodate the great event. Instead, an area of wasteland on the south side of the city was chosen, a site that offered ample space for the exhibition's Main Building and various additional pavilions. The rectangular Main Building, measuring 1,000 x 394 feet and built over a canal, faced the almost completed Rijksmuseum, the central underpass of which served as the main entrance to the site. The Colonial Pavilion was also partly built over water. These two buildings, combined with the Machinery Gallery, enclosed a landscaped, triangular area on which sat the smaller pavilions, including one for the city of Paris. In front of the Colonial Pavilion was a small settlement representing various overseas colonies. Most of the exhibition space was taken up by France and Belgium, followed by the Netherlands and Germany. The rest of the site served as an amusement park and was home to various foreign pavilions. At its focal point sat the Music Pavilion, itself surrounded by German, Dutch, and English restaurants.

Architectural purity At a time when there was fervent debate on architectural style in the Netherlands, the exhibition buildings received mixed reviews. At the core of the debate was the concept of architectural "truth." This boiled down to an argument over whether the exterior of buildings should reveal their functions and whether those exteriors should be stylistically pure – regardless of what style was chosen. The apogee of "honest" architecture – for at least one faction of Dutch architects – was the nearly completed Rijksmuseum, designed by P. J. H. Cuypers, which was incorporated into the exhibition and thereby gave a considerable boost to the allure of the small-scale event. Nevertheless, very few designs met with general approval. One that did was the façade of the Main Building, designed by the Frenchman Paul Fouquiau. Fouquiau's façade was a 164 foot-wide wood, plaster, and canvas wall with two, 82 foot-high towers at its ends. Suspended between the towers was a huge, drooping piece of canvas intended to resemble a cashmere shawl from the Orient. The building's other decorative motifs also evoked colonial outposts, and in this sense the exterior was in keeping with what was exhibited inside. The entire interior exhibition space was made of wood and canvas with iron supports, and had a total surface area of nearly 650,000 square feet. The design was by the Belgian Gédéon Bordiau, who also designed the Main Building at the 1885 Antwerp exhibition. If the Main Building was acceptable to critics, the Colonial Pavilion, with its Moorish minarets, was not. Critics pilloried it, attacking both the appropriateness of the building and the purity of its style.

The Dutch Renaissance style of the early seventeenth century was chosen for the remainder of the pavilions. It was during this period that the Dutch provinces developed into a strong bourgeois nation and freed themselves from the Spanish yoke. The Italianate Dutch Royal Pavilion, departing from this national style, was attacked by critics. Foreign pavilions that demonstrated their own national or regional histories earned general approval.

Overview of the exhibition site from the west with the international restaurants in the foreground. In contrast to what the plan suggests, it is evident that there was hardly any landscaping. Drawing by Johan Conrad Greive Jr.

Photograph of the exhibition site with the much criticized Colonial Pavilion (in center with minarets)

Interior of the Main Building

Like many of the fair's
buildings, the timbered
International Wine
Tavern was made of
wood

The exterior of the
Palace of Tunis

The Atjeh Monument
crowned by Victory –
somewhat premature
seeing that the battle it
commemorated was
still raging in the
Dutch East Indies

The Music Pavilion, sit-
uated amidst the inter-
national restaurants

The Colonial Village

The City of Amsterdam
Pavilion. The central
mural is by Johan A.
Rust

A visitor's opinion Pointed criticism came from "Osado," an employee of the architectural journal *De Opmerker*, who in several letters reported his own findings at the exhibition (and those of fictitious acquaintances he ran into at the event). "A more repugnantly tasteless hodgepodge of wood and canvas is inconceivable," claimed one "Nurks" in regard to the Dutch restaurant. In Osado's opinion, the Beaux-Arts pavilion was nothing but a hangar, and the site itself was as bleak as the Sahara. Osado did, however, enjoy the Amsterdam Pavilion (by the architect Adriaan Willem Weissman), the Royal Pavilion, and the waitresses of the German restaurant.

Following the exhibition, most of the fair's architecture was dismantled. The Main Building was sold in sections to the developers of the 1885 world's fair in Antwerp. After that event, parts were reused yet again for an exhibition in Liverpool.

Exposition Universelle d'Anvers Antwerp

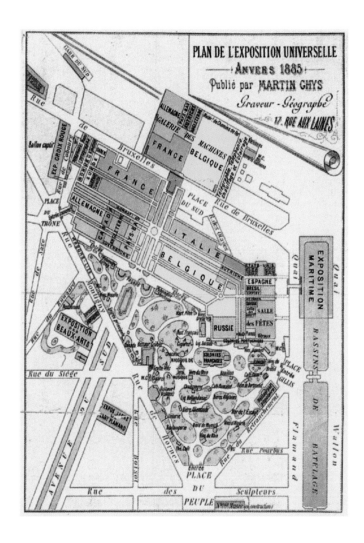

Façade of the Hall of
Decorative Arts

Map of the exhibition
site with the various
international sections in
color

Year **1885 (2 May – 2 November)** Location **Antwerp
(Het Zuid)** Surface area **54.3 acres** Attendance **3.5 million**
Participating nations **35** Exhibitors **14,472** Head of state **King
Leopold II** Chief architect **Gédéon Bordiau** Novelty **The
gas engine**

If the golden age of world's fairs had dawned in 1881 with the Sydney and Melbourne exhibitions, that age peaked in 1888, when no fewer than four were held simultaneously. Because these exhibitions were often hastily organized, arising from a desire to keep pace with other nations, architectural experimentation was not a primary concern, though the exhibitions were not necessarily uninteresting from an architectural perspective. Amsterdam 1883, for instance, was the first large international colonial exhibition. Antwerp 1885 proved that a small host country did not necessarily mean a small fair.

In comparison to the visual spectacle of later exhibitions, whose imaginative constructions bestowed them with lasting fame, the 1880s fairs have largely sunk into oblivion. This was the fate of the Antwerp world's fair of 1885, which was completely overshadowed by the Paris fair of 1889, with its stupendous Eiffel Tower. Nevertheless, Antwerp 1885 was the first in an impressive series of Belgian fairs: after Antwerp, exhibitions followed in Ghent, Liege, two more in Antwerp, and no fewer than five in Brussels.

The Hall of Decorative Arts under construction. In the foreground are the fair's smaller pavilions

The Thomas Cook & Son Pavilion

The Brazilian section in the Hall of Decorative Arts

Pavillon von Th. Cook & Son.

The site The exhibition was held on Het Zuid, an area set for urban development lying roughly on the former site of an old citadel and adjacent to the city's new harbor, the Scheldekaaien. The completion of the Scheldekaaien project served as the motivation for the mounting of the fair, and the surrounding area offered space in abundance. Ironically, the citadel and historic buildings of the old Sint Walburgsplein neighborhood had to be demolished to make way for the new Het Zuid development. Nine years later, the organizers of the Antwerp world's fair of 1894 were forced to create an ersatz Old Antwerp in wood and plaster.

Het Zuid was an easily accessible, trapezoidal site with a central avenue, the Zuidlaan, which led to the Hall of Decorative Arts. This hall, the main building of the exhibition, was linked to Machinery Hall and to another connecting building, all designed by Gédéon Bordiau. This was a disappointment for architect Jan Laurent Hasse, who was instrumental in the organization of the fair. To Hasse's dismay, the royal patron of the event, Leopold II, chose the court architect, Bordiau, in his place. A landscaped park was designed by the German-born Belgian Louis Fuchs. In its stylish gardens were the small pavilions of private companies and colonies, each a small cottage. Both Bordiau and Fuchs had worked for the Brussels Zoo, an experience that was put to good use; their eclectic cottage style sat well within the picturesque park, where the smaller pavilions acted as follies. These provided a contrast to the Hall of Decorative Arts, which was constructed of glass and iron, though ornamented in a kitsch style. Of particular note were the fair's many fountains and waterworks. The austere complex around the Hall of Decorative Arts and the Zuidlaan, however, was unrelated to the playful pavilions and the park in which they sat.

Design for the German
section in the Hall of
Decorative Arts, archi-
tect Grunert

Poster of the Antwerp
exhibition with the Hall
of Decorative Arts clear-
ly visible

Pavilion for the
Kemmerich Company
of St. Helena, Argentina

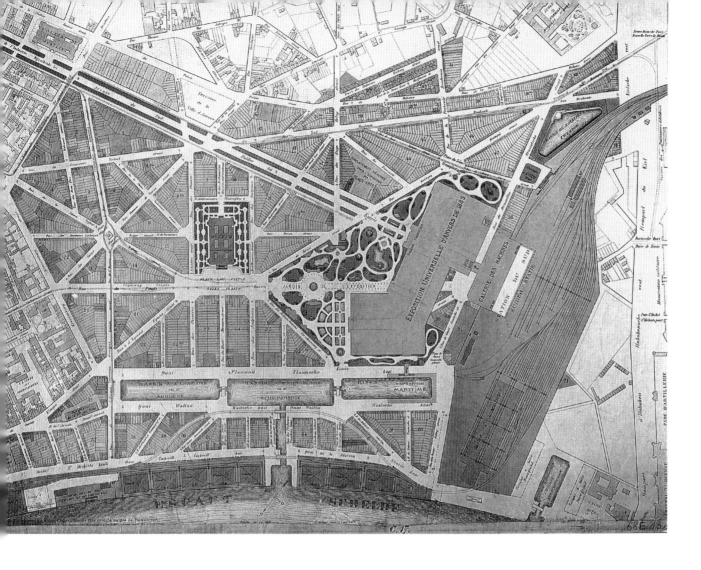

Map of the exhibition
site

The English section of
the Hall of Decorative
Arts

De Zoeten Inval
Pavilion restaurant

Buildings Hasse's failure to win the commission to design the main exhibition building meant he had to be content with a side entrance. He must therefore have observed with a certain perverse pleasure that Bordiau's main gate was still under scaffolding during the official opening of the exhibition; it was not completed until mid-July. Bordiau's entrance, intended as the visual focal point of the fair, consisted of an iron skeleton covered with imitation marble. Flanked by two lighthouses, it was a cross between a Roman triumphal arch and the mausoleum at Halicarnassus. At the top, at a height of 223 feet, was a globe supported by twelve statues of Atlas (the structure also housed a hydraulic elevator). Due to the exaggerated proportions of the entrance, the dome spanning the crossing of the Hall of Decorative Arts was completely obscured from the view of those entering the fair. That hall itself was composed of modular pieces so that after the exhibition closed the parts could be reused. These were not made of iron or glass, but from a combination of pressed stone, mortar, and cement, a mixture that could be used to simulate more expensive materials like granite and marble.

Parts of the 1885 exhibition, including the Zoeten Inval Pavilion, were allowed to remain standing until the Antwerp 1894 fair. If Antwerp 1885 was not an exceptional architectural event in itself, it did preview the structure that would become the great symbol of the world's fair. Displayed at the French stand were plans for a 984-foot tower by Gustave Eiffel. As for Jan Laurent Hasse, his practice thrived after 1885, and he would be a leading player at the Antwerp exhibition of 1894.

The Italian section in
the Hall of Decorative
Arts

Bird's-eye view of the
exhibition with the
Schelde in the back-
ground

French Colonies
Pavilion

Exposition Universelle Paris

The Eiffel Tower during
a light show

The Gas Industry
Pavilion on the
Champ de Mars

Year **1889 (6 May – 31 October)** Location **Paris (Champ de Mars, Trocadéro, banks of the Seine, Esplanade des Invalides)** Surface area **237 acres** Attendance **28,121,975** Exhibitors **61,722** Directeur Général des Travaux **Charles Adolph Alphand** Engineers **Gustave Eiffel, Victor Contamin** Architects **Joseph Bouvard, Jean-Camille Formigé, Charles Louis Ferdinand Dutert** Novelties **The Eiffel Tower, the phonograph**

The Paris Exposition Universelle of 1889 was a worthy conclusion to the long series of exhibitions held during the 1880s. Whereas the earlier exhibitions of that turbulent decade emanated a decadent eclecticism, at the Paris exhibition there were two constructions that can be seen as the successors of the Crystal Palace: the Eiffel Tower and the Galerie des Machines. That the latter was dismantled in 1910 is an inestimable loss to France's capital city and to the world.

The chief reason for holding the Exhibition Universelle was to commemorate the centennial of the storming of the Bastille and the French Revolution. But for many European royals such a subversive anniversary was reason *not* to attend the event, or to simply send an official delegation (foreign leaders were also concerned about potential political unrest stemming from the theme). Though there were seven thousand official foreign exhibitors at the fair, the event proved more national than international. Notwithstanding, Paris 1889 was a resounding success, and when it closed its 32.3 million visitors had even left the organizers with a tidy profit.

World's Fairs

**Plan of the Esplanade
des Invalides**

**Plan of the Colonial
Exhibition on
the Esplanade des
Invalides site**

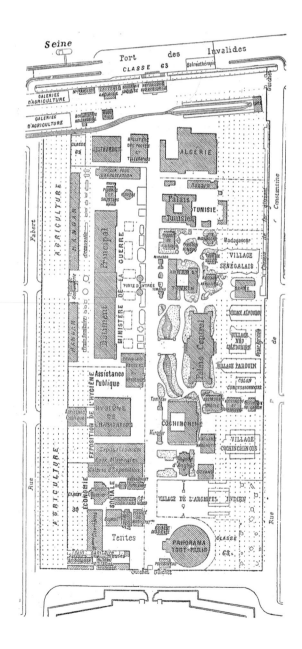

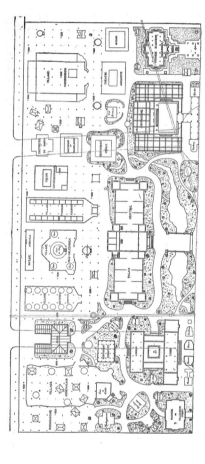

The foundations of the
Eiffel Tower

Plan of the exhibition site

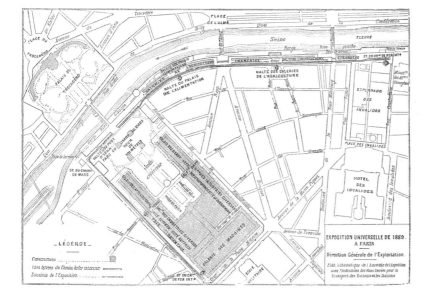

Site and Main Building Just as in 1878, the exhibition was held on the Champ de Mars and the

Trocadéro. A Colonial Exhibition was also mounted on the Esplanade des Invalides. The Champ de Mars and the
Esplanade were linked by the south bank of the Seine, where the Hall of Agriculture and the Palais des Alimentations
were to be found amongst other fair buildings. The curved arms of the Trocadéro together with the wings of the Palais
des Industries Diverses (across the Seine on the Champ de Mars) formed an enclosed, landscaped setting. Within this
space were several national pavilions and the 984-foot (300 meter) Eiffel Tower, which stood in the center of the park
like a gigantic folly. The central axis of the exhibition ran directly under the tower, through the park, and straight toward
the entrance of the Main Building.

This building, like that for Antwerp 1885 and for many other exhibitions, was a series of interconnected small galleries. The wings of the main building ran into the Palais des Beaux Arts and the Palais des Arts Décoratifs, respectively.
These palaces were massive, hall-shaped structures constructed of iron, each bearing a central dome. Noteworthy was
the use of terra cotta as a building material. The architect of the Main Building was Jean-Camille Formigé; the entrance,
a pompous domed structure, was designed by Joseph Bouvard. At the rear of the rear Main Building was the magnificent
Galerie des Machines.

Galerie des Machines

With a span of 375 feet, the Galerie des Machines, designed by engineer Victor Contamin and architect Charles Louis Ferdinand Dutert, represented a high point in the history of modern construction and a logical step in the development of Parisian exhibition design. The crucial problem was, as always, how to cover the greatest possible space without resorting to a forest of internal columns for support. Contamin's solution was to create a framework whose thrust was directed down to the ground – not out to the sides, which would have required buttressing. Massive hinged trusses tapered as they fell from the roof, allowing the structure to rest on improbably thin legs. In addition to its creative spanning technique, the structure was remarkably easy to build. The skin of the Galerie was mainly glass, revealing the entire structural system, and the whole was completed in barely six months. The machinery exhibits could be viewed from electrically driven moving platforms (*ponts roulants*) suspended over the hall. The primary building material was cast iron: although available, steel was still too expensive, stone more costly still. Instead, construction cost just eight million francs, the same as the Eiffel Tower.

The Palais des Produits Alimentaires and (on the left) the Portugese Pavilion

Bird's-eye view of the Champ de Mars

Entrance to the Galerie des Machines

Plan of the Champ de Mars

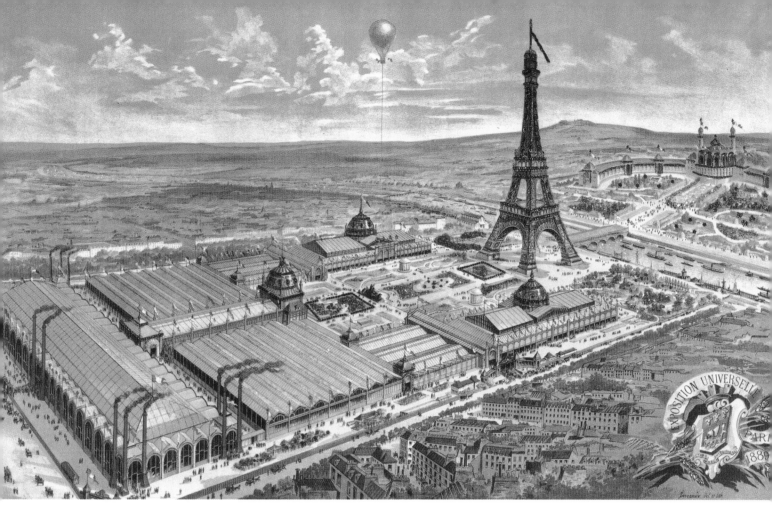

part à assurer la paix de l'Europe, puisque nous, que le chancelier de paix représente toujours comme prêts à déchaîner la guerre, nous prendrions l'engagement moral de

Le 8 novembre 1884, le Président de la République, M. Jules Grévy, signa donc, sur le rapport de M. Rouvier, ministre du Commerce, un décret portant qu'une Expo-

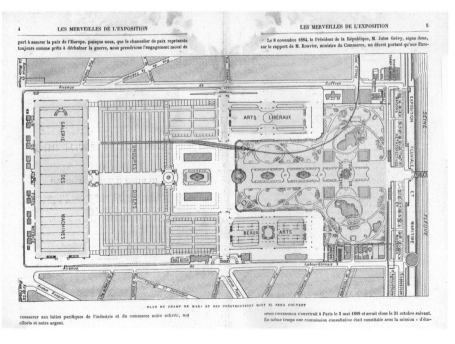

PLAN DU CHAMP DE MARS ET DES CONSTRUCTIONS DONT IL SERA COUVERT

consacrer aux luttes pacifiques de l'industrie et du commerce notre activité, nos efforts et notre argent.

sition universelle s'ouvrirait à Paris le 5 mai 1889 et serait close le 31 octobre suivant. En même temps une commission consultative était constituée avec la mission « d'étu-

The Public Works
Pavilion

The Eiffel Tower under
construction with the
Trocadéro in the back-
ground

The Maritime Pavilion,
part of the separate
Maritime Exhibition

The exhibition site
could be reached via a
footbridge at the Pont
de l'Alma

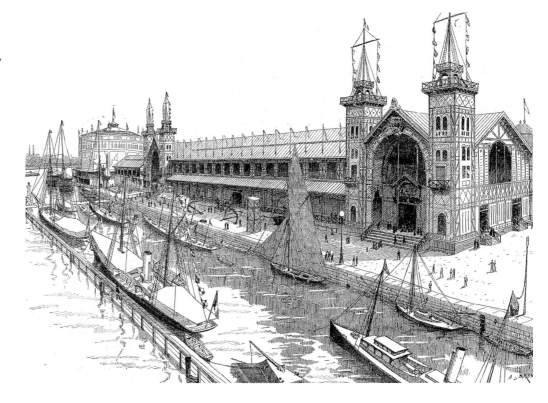

The Eiffel Tower The fact that the Eiffel Tower was initially considered monstrous and unsightly by painters, architects, and sculptors is telling of the artistic climate of *fin-de-siecle* Paris. A cast-iron structure without walls, roof, or dome towering over the city was deemed entirely inappropriate by a great many Parisians. In this light, Gustave Eiffel's achievement is all the more remarkable; his tower was both a technological and a political feat. Like many other exhibition buildings, the tower was the product of a competition. Eiffel, however, had a head start in that he had already submitted a design, conceived by engineers in his employ – Maurice Koechlin and Emile Nouguier – in 1884. The tower was given structural rigidity by a network of girders, the force of wind reducedby tapering the tower toward its apex and by anchoring it to a giant reinforced concrete foundation. The semicircular arches separating the legs are actually decorative, not part of the structural support system. Architectural detailing, was by architect Stephen Sauvestre. Eiffel had his own apartment at the very top of the tower, and there were restaurants below. Construction lasted from January 1887 to March 1889, and when completed the tower was illuminated by gaslights from top to bottom. The Eiffel Tower consists of 1,050,846 rivets for which seven million holes were drilled.

Habitation Humaine   A fixed component of world's fairs was the recreation of existing building types in a picturesque village. Theoretically intended as an educational environment, in practice such villages were just as much amusements. At the suggestion of Charles Garnier, the still influential architect of the Paris Opéra, one of two thematic exhibitions was devoted to human dwellings. Sited at the foot of the Eiffel Tower – a structure Garnier detested – fifty abodes revealed the history of shelter from the Stone Age to the present day.

A variation on the picturesque village was a complete reconstruction in wood and plaster of the Bastille and its immediate surroundings. In contrast to this display of French republicanism was the Colonial Exhibition, a collection of recreated dwellings and complete villages – including inhabitants – plundered from France's overseas colonies. The foreign pavilions, built in national styles, were scattered throughout the exhibition site. The Swedish Pavilion has even withstood the test of time. After the exhibition it was dismantled and shipped back to its homeland.

The Galerie des
Machines under
construction

Gustave Eiffel's
apartment high up in
the Eiffel Tower

Houses in the
Habitation Humaine
section

Interior of the Galerie
des Machines

Assembling the trusses
of the Galerie des
Machines. The arched
trusses are linked by
iron hinges

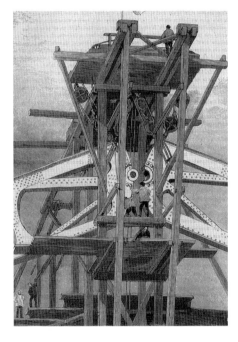

The Chemin de Fer Glissant or "gliding railway" (actually a small train powered by water pressure) connected the Galerie des Machines and the Esplanade des Invalides

Hector Guimard's pavilion for "electrotherapist" Ferdinand de Boyères

Other buildings

The Trocadéro, built for the 1878 Exposition Universelle, housed the horticulture exhibits. Newly constructed were pavilions for agriculture, maritime, hygiene, gas, electricity, the city of Paris, and other official institutions. There were also pavilions for private associations such as the Watercolorists and Pastellists. Though Paris 1889 achieved fame for its two great modern constructions, most of the pavilions at the fair were in the prevailing style of the time – a heavily accentuated classical eclecticism – though new materials like glass and iron were in evidence. This conservatism was also demonstrated by the art sanctioned for display: the art of the French academy. Impressionist painters were excluded.

There were, however, signs at Paris 1889 of a nascent style that would emerge at the Brussels exhibition of 1897 and flower at the Paris fair of 1900: art nouveau. The applied arts section of the 1889 fair presented glass work by Emile Gallé, and one of the smaller pavilions at the exhibition was designed by the young architect Hector Guimard – only his second completed commission.

With Paris 1889 the nature of the world's fair changed. The trade fair, with the aim of finding new outlets for new products, had become an object of history. Henceforth, exhibitions would be of a more recreational character, their goal to entertain a broad, popular audience. The underlying idea that holding such international gatherings would bolster world peace remained. In the twentieth century, even this would disappear.

The Brazilian Pavilion
on the Champ de Mars

Façade of the Grande
Galerie Centrale in the
Main Building

Interior of the Grande
Galerie Centrale

World's Columbian Exposition Chicago

The colonnade of Machinery Hall, architects Peabody & Stearns

Bird's-eye view of the exhibition site

Year **1893 (1 May – 31 October)** Location **Chicago (Jackson Park)** Surface area **686 acres** Attendance **27.3 million** Participating nations **50** Exhibitors **50,000** Chief of Construction **Daniel H. Burnham** Novelties **Hand-held cameras, the radio**

The 1893 World's Columbian Exposition was held to commemorate of the discovery of the New World by Christopher Columbus in 1492. The fact that the festivities took place 401 instead of four hundred years after this date can be attributed to delays in the preparatory phase of exhibition planning. Various American cities fought over the honor to host the prestigious event (New York, St. Louis, and Washington were Chicago's chief competitors) before Congress – after eight years of indecision – finally awarded the event to Chicago. This was a major victory for the booming city, which sought to rid itself of the provincial label bestowed on it by its great East Coast rivals. Similarly, the fair would allow the entire American nation to shed a sense of cultural inferiority long held in regard to Europe. By surpassing the great exhibitions of Paris, the Columbian Exposition would establish both the host city and the host country as economic and cultural powers.

The Site In 1890 the distinguished landscape architect Frederick Law Olmsted, who had been developing a park along a marshy strip of land between Chicago and Lake Michigan since 1871, drew up a report in which he proposed that this site be used for the exhibition. The various commissions overseeing the event agreed, and Olmsted was appointed its supervising landscape architect. In turn, Olmsted left much of the design work in the hands of his dynamic young assistant, Henry S. Codman. Meanwhile, the Chicago architectural office of Burnham & Root was chosen to oversee the design of the fair's buildings. Together, Olmsted, Codman, John W. Root, and Daniel H. Burnham split the site into quadrants, at once making the immense tract manageable. The exhibition was formally arranged around a symmetrical pool, the Court of Honor; various international pavilions were situated about an asymmetric area; there was a scenic lagoon; and fairground attractions were removed to the Midway, a strip running perpendicular to the main exhibition site. The terrain between the buildings was spacious enough to allow for circulation and to enable the general public to admire the exhibition's buildings from a sufficiently grand distance (visitors could even rent hand-held cameras for two dollars per day).

The Women's Building, architect Sophia Hayden

Main entrance to the Agriculture Building, architects Mckim, Mead & White

Buildings After Root's premature death in 1891, Burnham assumed full control over the fair's building program. His first decision was a generous one. Instead of keeping all of the commissions for his own firm – a massive task for one office – he decided several architects were required. He did not, however, hold a competition. Instead, Burnham awarded the prized commissions for the buildings on the Court of Honor to a group of highly distinguished architects largely from the East Coast. The exclusion of Chicago firms from this list caused much bitterness, and has been seen as pivotal in the history of American architecture. Burnham's position was nothing if not delicate: he was obligated to choose from the New York-based architectural establishment (he had to answer to a national committee nervous about Chicago's supposed provincialism); the architects he chose had to represent the various regions of a united nation (the Civil War still weighed on the American conscience); and he wanted architects capable of a stylistically unified architectural statement that would eclipse any European precedent. Regardless of its effect on the future of American architecture (and on the fate of his local competitors), Burnham's choice of École des Beaux Arts-trained architects from the East (and one from St. Louis) satisfied these obligations.

The architects Burnham tagged were Richard Morris Hunt, the so-called dean of American architecture, for the centerpiece Administration Building; George B. Post for the Manufactures and Liberal Arts Building; Van Brunt & Howe for the Electricity Building; Peabody & Sterns for Machinery Hall; and McKim, Mead & White for the Agriculture Building. In response to the controversy, Burnham was forced to hire Chicago architects for lesser commissions. These included: Solon S. Beman (Mines and Mining); William Le Baron Jenney (Horticulture); and Louis Sullivan (Transportation). The prestigious Palace of Fine Arts, on the north side of the Lagoon, was awarded to Burnham's new associate Charles Atwood, who was to design some sixty structures for the exhibition, including the Peristyle, a series of thirteen columns (representing the founding colonies) enclosing the Court of Honor. Sophia Hayden designed the Women's Building, though many women objected to being ostracized with a separate structure.

In a New York meeting attended only by the prestigious East Coast group – without Burnham – it was decided that the buildings would be designed in a uniform neoclassical style with fixed cornice lines and dimensions. All construction and decoration at the fair would adhere to this style. The buildings were to be covered with staff, a bright white plaster mixture, so they would appear as marble. Thus the fair came to be known as the "White City."

Transportation
Building, architect
Louis H. Sullivan

The Court of Honor
with Daniel Chester
French's *Statue of the
Republic* in the fore-
ground, McKim, Mead
& White's Agriculture
Building at left, Richard
Morris Hunt's
Administration building
in the distance, and
George B. Post's
Manufactures and
Liberal Arts Building at
right. The well-known
image is by official fair
photographer C. D.
Arnold

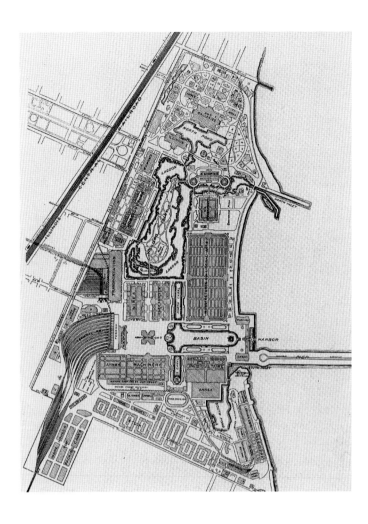

Plan of the exhibition
site

Interior of the
Manufactures and
Liberal Arts Building

Administration Building
with Machinery Hall on
the left

Manufactures and
Liberal Arts Building

The Electricity Building
seen from the north,
architects Van Brunt &
Howe

The Agriculture
Building

The Swedish Pavilion,
architect Ferdinand
Boberg

Cover of a picture
album issued to com-
memorate the fair

The Fisheries Pavilion,
architect Henry Ives
Cobb

The Lagoon with the
dome of William Le
Baron Jenney's
Horticulture Building in
the distance

The entrance to the
Transportation Building

Classicism in America   Classicism, as exemplified by the Columbian Exposition, struck a positive chord with the American public and became the country's *de facto* national style, as seen in countless governmental buildings and civic works. It was at this time that the American Academy of Rome was established, its aim to undertake further research into classical architecture and the continuity of neoclassicism. The conservatism of this architecture has long been a subject of criticism. While skyscrapers of the most advanced design were mushrooming in Chicago, the Columbian Exposition was largely closed to the architectural world around it.

The *Columbian
Fountain* by Frederick
William MacMonies

Lagoon seen from the
Southern Canal

The exhibition
The Columbian Exposition, with participants from no fewer than fifty nations, was huge in every sense of the word. Logistically, the event was well organized. A small electric train transported visitors around the site via a looping track, and a rudimentary moving sidewalk carried fairgoers from entry pier to fairgrounds. The fair was also a major factor in Chicago's decision to create its metro system, the fourth in the world. Though electricity was becoming a commonplace, the fair's large-scale application of it was unique; in the evening, the buildings were dazzlingly illuminated. In the event of a short circuit, the exhibition's own fire brigade came to the rescue. Every type of service was available to attendees, including telephone and telegraph. The fair was heavily policed, and a sanitation crew made the entire site spotless every night.

The Midway fairgrounds featured the original Ferris Wheel, George Ferris's 260-foot answer to the Eiffel Tower and one of the icons of the fair. The Midway was also the location of the fair's ethnological exhibitions – including an "Esquimaux Village" and a "Native American Show." Controversy erupted when Innuits complained of gross mistreatment and exploitation. If the inclusion of such exhibits seems disturbing today, equally troubling is the exclusion of African-Americans from participation in the fair. This prompted the publication of the treatise *The Reason Why. The Colored American is not in the Columbian Exposition*, coauthored by Frederick Douglass.

German section of the
Manufactures and
Liberal Arts Building

Machinery Hall

The Horticulture
Building

Palace of Fine Arts,
architect Charles B.
Atwood

L'EXPOSITION
DE
PARIS 1900

Exposition Universelle Paris

Title page of the official fair catalog with, in the foreground, the Porte Monumentale (Porte Binet)

One of two monumental conservatories on the bank of the Seine

Year **1900 (14 April – 12 November)** Location **Paris (Champ de Mars, Trocadéro, Esplanades des Invalides, Avenue Alexandre III, Bois de Vincennes)** Surface area **543 acres** Attendance **48 million** Exhibitors **76,112** Director **Alfred Picard** Chief Architect **Joseph-Antoine Bouvard** Novelties **Escalators, The Olympic Games, panoramic movies**

Both Germany and France hoped to hold the prestigious fair that would mark the turn of the century. Germany had never hosted an international exhibition, and the occasion seemed a suitably grand opportunity. But when the German delegation realized there was no hope of having the event prepared on schedule, Paris became the more-than-willing host of its fifth fair in just forty-five years. In addition to the Exposition Universelle, it also hosted the second modern Olympic Games, held in the Bois de Vincennes as a special attraction of the exhibition. Record-setting attendance was anticipated.

Site   If the Bois de Vincennes is included – the Olympics and several exhibition pavilions were located there – Paris 1900 is the largest exhibition ever held in Europe. The main site was, as usual, the Champ de Mars and the Trocadéro, and this was extended toward the Place de la Concorde. On the right bank, the old Palais de l'Industrie from the 1855 fair was considered unsuitable and was taken down. In its place rose the Musée Centénal, the Palais des Beaux Arts (the Grand Palais), the Palais des Arts Rétrospectives (the Petit Palais), and the fair's two main gates, the Porte d'Honneur and the Porte Monumentale. The former was situated on the Avenue Triomphale, the main axis of the fair, the latter – known as the Porte Binet, after its architect, René Binet – was positioned along the Seine. The Avenue Triomphale ran to the Pont Alexandre III – specially built for the occasion – across the river, and to the Esplanade des Invalides, where a huge complex was devoted to the applied arts: the Palais de l'Esplanade des Invalides. Both banks of the Seine were incorporated into the exhibition. Along its left bank was the Rue des Nations, a stretch of foreign pavilions each in its own style. Picturesque Old Paris also fronted the river.

The Porte Monumentale
seen from the Place de
la Concorde

LA PORTE MONUMENTALE SUR LA PLACE DE LA CONCORDE

The Chateau d'Eau, designed by Gustave Raulin and Eugène A. Henard, was one of the exhibition's major attractions and was situated in a courtyard on the Champ de Mars

Richard Riemerschmid's design for an interior on display in the German installation

The Galerie des Machines of 1889 was totally rebuilt and became the rear of an enormous exhibition building complex. At the foot of the Eiffel Tower were various thematic pavilions; the French colonial pavilions were sited in the Trocadéro garden. The entire exhibition area was so large that to view all the products of one nation a spectator would have to cover many miles. Facilitating this was a two-speed moving sidewalk – the Trottoir Roulant – that looped the main sites at 2.25 and 4.5 miles-per-hour. The exhibition also accelerated the development of the Paris Métro. The first line constructed had twenty-three stations and two branch lines – including one to the Trocadéro – and ran from Porte Maillot to Porte de Vincennes.

Architecture

Whereas the Paris 1889 exhibition was a triumph for the engineer, the Beaux-Arts trained architect returned with a vengeance in 1900. If nineteenth-century fairs had often served as laboratories for new styles and advanced technology, at this exhibition the vanguard architecture of H. J. P. Berlage, Victor Horta, Joseph Olbrich, and Henry Van de Velde was assigned only a supporting role. With few exceptions, the buildings were coated with plaster – as they were at the Columbian Exposition seven years earlier – obscuring their methods of construction, pretending to be that which they were not. The elegant work of engineers Louis Résal and Jules Alby on the Pont Alexandre III, with its span of 350 feet, was subordinated to the ostentatious design of architects Marie Joseph Cassien-Bernard and Gaston Clément Cousin and the flamboyant sculptural work of Georges Recipon. The splendid Galerie des Machines of 1889 was transformed by Gustave Raulin into an extravagantly decorated showpiece: a banqueting hall for 25,000 topped by a dome with a diameter of roughly 300 feet. Plans to give the Eiffel Tower a facelift were fortunately abandoned, though its gas lighting was replaced by some 5,000 electric lamps and it was painted yellow. The glass and metal roof of the Grand Palais was a superb feat of engineering artistry, but the building's façade was a disappointing Louis XIV pastiche

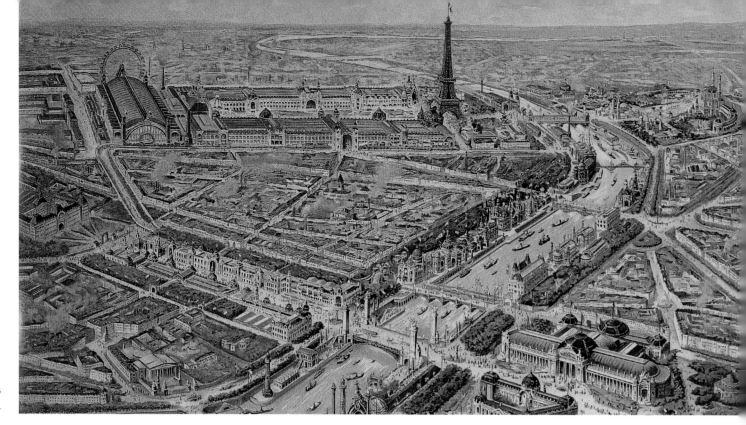

Bird's-eye view of the
exhibition site. The
Esplanade des Invalides
is linked with the Grand
Palais and Petit Palais.
A footbridge is visible
in an upper bend of the
Seine

Plan of the exhibition
site. An electric train
and a moving sidewalk
ran in a loop between
the two exhibition areas

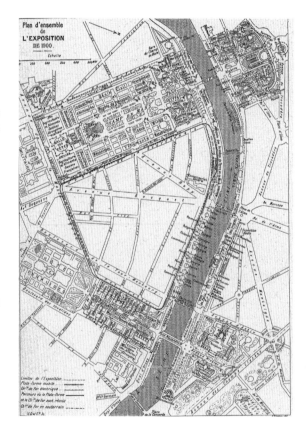

The Loïe Fuller Theater, architect Henri Sauvage assisted by Francis Jourdain and Pierre Roche

Entrance to the Palais des Manufactures on the Esplanade des Invalides, architects Toudoire & Pradelle

Poster for the Loïe Fuller Theater by Manuel Orazi

An artist's impression of the newly completed Banqueting Hall – the former Galerie des Machines – designed by Gustave Raulin. Watercolor by Georges Garen

It is all too easy, however, to see the Paris 1900 exhibition as a triumph of historicism in general and of neo-Louis styles in particular. At the turn of the century, European architecture was rapidly evolving and there was a general search for a new formal language. At the 1897 world exhibition in Brussels, the Belgian architects Paul Hankar, Victor Horta, and Henry Van de Velde had created art nouveau interiors for pavilions. In their fervor to produce something different for the 1900 fair, architects plundered so many historical types for inspiration that they created a new, bizarre type of eclecticism in which the various styles were fused in such away that their original forms became unrecognizable. The best example of this style is the Chateau d'Eau, an odd reinforced concrete construction designed by Raulin and Eugène A. Hénard. The Porte Binet, the Porte des Invalides, and the entrances to the Palais des Lettres, Sciences et Arts, may also be included in this exuberant style. Most foreign entries did not venture beyond the reproduction of buildings from their own histories. Belgium, for instance, recreated the town hall in Oudenaarde; America remained true to the classicism that had emerged at the Chicago 1893 exhibition; and Britain, under the direction of Edwin Lutyens, reproduced the Hall at Bradford-on-Avon.

Monumental entrance
to the port of the Palais
du Champ de Mars,
architect Sortais

International pavilions
on the bank of the
Seine, seen from the
Pont de l'Alma

Grand Palais (Albert
Félix Thomas, Henri
Dèglane, and Albert
Louvet) and Petit Palais
(Charles Girault) with
the Pont Alexandre III
in the foreground

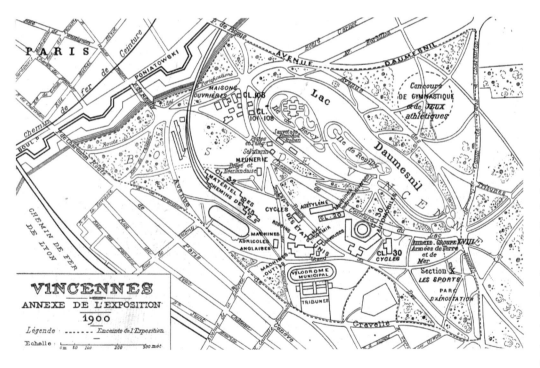

Main entrance of the
Palais du Génie Civil
(part of the Palais du
Champ de Mars),
architect Jacques
Hermant

The Finnish Pavilion,
architect Eliel Saarinen

The Parc Vincennes,
designated for the sec-
ond Olympic Games,
was best reached via
the new Métro

Palais des Invalides
Manufactures
Nationales on the
Esplanades des
Invalides seen from
Pont Alexandre III,
architects Toudoire &
Pradelle. This building
complex took up almost
the entire Esplanade
des Invalides

The moving sidewalk
provided a means of get-
ting from one section of
the exhibition site to
another

Design for a Perfume
Pavilion by Frantz
Jourdain

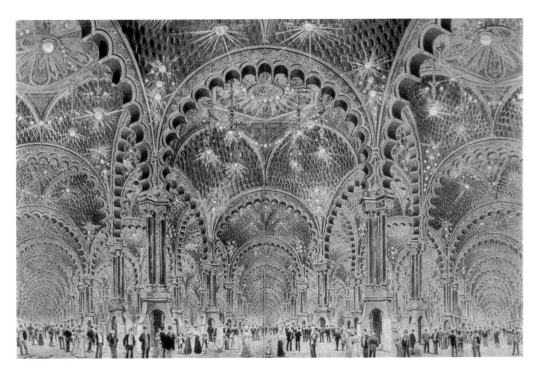

The Salle des Illusions between the Banqueting Hall and the Palais de l'Electricité, architect Eugène A. Henard

The Pont d'Alma with the Palais des Congrès in the background

The Palais des Invalides, rue de Grénelle. Architect Tropey-Bailly

Poster for the new Métro with an entrances designed by Hector Guimard

Other trends   There were other styles on exhibition. Situated along the Seine, Ferdinand Boberg's Swedish Pavilion stood out with its bright red and yellow tones and stacked volumes. The Finnish Pavilion, by Eliel Saarinen, was similarly striking, though it was not recognized as such at the time; the only description of it in a catalog of the fair's buildings, for instance, pointed out that it was based on a Finnish village church. Dazed, apparently, by the surfeit of pavilion styles, the catalog's author failed to fully appreciate Saarinen's restrained formal vocabulary. Of the French pavilions that deviated from the prevailing style, the architects responsible belonged to the circle of architect Frantz Jourdain. Henri Sauvage, now recognized as one of Paris's foremost modern architects, designed the Majorelle Pavilion and the Fuller Pavilion, the latter in collaboration with the sculptor Pierre Roche. Still Paris landmarks today, Hector Guimard's Métro entrances drew much attention at the time. Originally, more classically-oriented architects were sought for this commission. But Guimard won the job, and soon became one of Europe's most prominent architects.

Interiors   The interiors of the international pavilions were every bit as original and inventive as their exteriors were conservative. Free of the restraining straightjacket of historicism and unimpeded by the physical laws of structure, design flowered. Furniture, accessories, and interiors by Olbrich, Berlage, Josef Hoffmann, Richard Riemerschmid, Bruno Paul, Josef Fanta, and Alphonse Mucha, appeared. Noticeable by their absence were Van de Velde, Horta, and Charles Rennie Mackintosh. The new art, however, like the more eclectic architecture, was not without its excesses. Sinuous forms and elegant materials often meant costly designs.

The Blue Pavilion restaurant by Réne Dulong with Gustave Serrurier-Bovy was one of the few art nouveau pavilions

Interior of the Blue Pavilion, Réne Dulong

Interior of the Grand
Palais

Art dealer Samuel
Bing's pavilion, archi-
tect Georges de Feure

Implications The search for a new style, typical of every architectural generation, manifested itself at the turn of the century in both the exaggerated language of eclecticism and in the forms of art nouveau. Critically, the architecture of the exhibition was not well received. Just eleven years after the Eiffel Tower had been derided as a bare industrial eyesore, the press deemed the pavilions of the 1900 fair tastelessly extravagant confections. Despite hosting fifty million visitors, negative criticism – along with slim profits for exhibitors – have left it somewhat poorly served by history. But the fair left a lasting mark on Paris, and its shift in focus toward the decorative arts reflected a continuing evolution of the world's fair away from its industrial roots.

Esposizione d'Arte Decorativa Moderna

Turin

The Music Pavilion,
architect Raimondo
d'Aronco

La Rotonda d'Onore,
architect Raimondo
d'Aronco

Year **1902 (10 May – 10 November)** Location **Turin (Parco del Valentino)** Participating nations **13** Honorary president **Walter Crane** Chief architect **Raimondo d'Aronco** Project manager **Ernesto Bonelli** Artistic director **Annibale Rigotti** Decorator **Giovanni Vacchetta**

The Turin 1902 exhibition was the first for the newly unified Italian state and was soon followed by smaller exhibitions in Milan (1906) and Rome (1911). The series culminated with the dubious Esposizione Universale di Roma of 1942, organized for the greater glory of the fascist regime.

Raimondo d'Aronco
The architectural design for the exhibition was chiefly determined by one of the most imaginative Italian architects of the turn of the century: Raimondo d'Aronco. Around this time he had his office in Constantinople where he devoted his efforts to that earthquake-struck city. When he heard in 1900 of a competition for the main pavilion of the exhibition, he submitted a design that was chosen immediately. His first design was rather historicist in style and was quickly replaced by a new proposal that was even more enthusiastically received than the previous one. The organizing committee, which had elevated the artists' colony of Darmstadt to the level of an ideal, was resolute that only the new art and architecture be shown and that historical styles be avoided at all costs. Highly satisfied, with d'Aronco's design for the Rotunda, the committee awarded the architect, who was still living abroad, one commission after another.
He went on to design the various pavilions with unbridled dedication and in his letters he instructed the on-site supervisor, with his other wishes for his design. D'Aronco was extremely disappointed on arriving at the site prior to the opening, when he found that not everything had been executed as he had wanted. Unfortunately nothing remains of D'Aronco's exhibition architecture and an idea of his idiosyncratic style can only be gained from drawings and photographs. The Rotunda featured a dome modeted on the Hagia Sofia. The other pavilions and the entrance, which were designed after the Rotunda, also diverged in style from standard modes. The entrance to the photography pavilion, for instance, was similar in form to a giant aperture. It is almost impossible to believe that in such a short space of time – the Automobile Pavilion was designed in just one week – someone could produce such a body of totally original work. During the exhibition itself d'Aronco's genius was barely recognized and only his Turkish pavilion found any real favor. One of the reasons for this is that critics so revered Olbrich that other architects were considered slavish imitators or, as in the case of architect Peter Behrens who designed the German section, merely second rate.

The Automobile pavilion, architect Raimondo d'Aronco

Design for the Main Entrance, architect Raimondo d'Aronco. The bull depicted on the banner is the symbol of Turin

Dining room by Joseph Olbrich. More than Peter Behrens, Olbrich was considered the foremost applied artists within the German-speaking countries

Design for the Automobile Pavilion

Interior of the Hamburger vestibule, architect Peter Behrens

Louisiana Purchase Exposition St. Louis

Cass Gilbert's Festival Hall with E. L. Masqueray's Cascades in the foreground

Photograph of the exhibition at sunset by Jessie Tarbox Beals

Year **1904 (30 April – 1 December)** Location **St. Louis, Forest Park** Surface area **1,272 acres** Visitors **19,694,855** Head of State **Theodore Roosevelt** Fair President **David R. Francis** Director of Works **Isaac S. Taylor** Chief of Design **E. L. Masqueray** Novelties **The ice cream cone, iced tea**

At the turn of the century St. Louis was the fourth-largest city in the United States and expanding rapidly. Only recently a frontier outpost, it had become the so-called gateway to the American West. In 1893, St. Louis's great rival to the north, Chicago, had hosted the mammoth Columbian Exposition, in the process establishing itself as a city of international import. By hosting its own fair, St. Louis would keep pace with Chicago and mark its own presence on the world stage. The pretext for the event was the centennial of the 1803 signing of the Louisiana Purchase Agreement between France and the United States (the exhibition opened a year late); the driving force behind it was David R. Francis, St. Louis's leading citizen, a former mayor of the city and governor of Missouri.

The site Forest Park, a heavily wooded park in the path of the city's development, was chosen as the site for the event. It was not an uncontroversial decision; many St. Louis citizens objected to the clearing of the park, known as the "Wilderness." Nevertheless, the transformation went forward, though work proved difficult. The Des Peres, a sewage-ridden river with a penchant for flooding, snaked through the park and had to be rechanneled and moved underground. St. Louis was also forced to invest heavily in its water system in order to provide a potable supply to both the exhibition and its citizens. As many as fifteen-thousand laborers worked daily to transform the massive park area to a suitable fairgrounds.

The main buildings were arranged in a radiating plan devised by New York architect Cass Gilbert (who would achieve fame as the architect of the Woolworth Building) and Frank M. Howe of Kansas City (the one non-East Coast representative on the architectural commission of the Columbian Exposition). In practice, it was quite similar to the Chicago 1893 plan: the focal point was Cass Gilbert's domed and ornate Festival Hall, which sat elevated on Art Hill. In front of this was the Cascades, a light-studded waterworks – designed by the fair's chief of design, E. L. Masqueray – that demonstrated the city's mastery over the natural element that so challenged it. The Cascades ran down to the oblong Grand

The United States Government Building, architect James Knox Taylor. On the left is Barnett, Haynes & Barnett's Palace of Liberal Arts

The Missouri Corn Palace offered a contrast to the seriousness of the fair's architecture

Basin, on either side of which were arrayed the main exhibition buildings. These separated the states pavilions (grouped on the Plateau of States) from the foreign pavilions and the venues for the sparsely attended Olympic Games, which were held concurrently as part of the exhibition.

Behind the main buildings were the fair's amusements, which included a 13-acre reproduction of the city of Jerusalem (including Church of the Holy Sepulchre, Dome of the Rock, and Western Wall), and the gigantic, Philippine Reservation. The latter, encompassing 47 acres, was populated by seven "primitive" Philippine tribes and exhibits demonstrating the fruits of America's most prized colonial possession. Other attractions along the Pike (St. Louis's answer to Chicago's Midway) were the Tyrolean Alps (with a restaurant run by New Yorker August Lüchow), Hagenbeck's Zoological Paradise (with its elephant slide), and the Ferris Wheel (also imported from Chicago). Fairgoers could navigate the grounds via the Intramural Railway, which departed from the Transportation Building,

Architecture   As with the Columbian exhibition, the temporary buildings of the Louisiana Purchase Exposition were designed in a uniform Beaux-Arts style. Painted white, most had timber frameworks covered over with staff. With the Chicago fair known as the "White City," the St. Louis exhibition was dubbed the "Ivory City." Notable among the exhibition buildings were Masqueray's Palace of Transportation, with its three arched entries and profuse ornament; Walker & Kimball's Palace of Electricity, on which Thomas Edison served as chief consulting engineer; and Carrère and Hastings' massive Palace of Manufactures, which covered roughly 14 acres and was divided in two by a circular court (with hardware on one side and textiles on the other). Many of the foreign pavilions were recreations of landmark buildings: the German installation was a reproduction of the Palace of Charlottenburg, the French Pavilion a facsimile of the Grand Trianon of Versailles. The Austrian entry, which was singled out for an award by the exhibition's Arts Committee, was the most progressive of these, a product of the Vienna Secession movement.

Only one building from the fair remains standing today, Cass Gilbert's Palace of Fine Arts, now the St. Louis Art Museum. The exhibition, however, was forever memorialized in the film musical *Meet Me in St. Louis*, starring Judy Garland.

The entrance to the
"Creation" installation
on the Pike. Inside, the
creation myth from
Genesis was enacted
and a diorama depicted
man's progress to
civilization

French exhibition
poster by Alphonse
Mucha

Interior of the award-
winning Austrian
Pavilion

Exposition Universelle et Internationale

Brussels

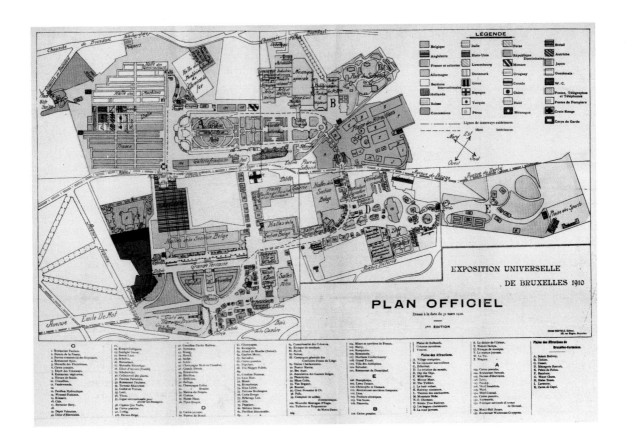

Original design by
Willem Kromhout for
the Dutch Pavilion
(1908)

Map of the exhibition
site

Year **1910**   Location **Brussels**   Surface area **217.4 acres**
Visitors **13 million**   Participating nations **26**   Head of state
Albert I

If art nouveau had flowered at the Turin fair of 1902, eight years later, in the land of Henri Van de Velde, Victor Horta, and Paul Hankar, overwrought historicist styles once again prevailed. Belgium paid dearly for betraying its art nouveau heritage, however. During the fair, on the afternoon of August 14, the Grand Palais, the exhibition's main building, burned to the ground leaving a pile of blackened and twisted iron at the heart of the site (a new building was quickly erected in the same eclectic style). The general historicist flavor of the fair has led many critics to discount its importance. Yet Brussels 1910 was an interesting exhibition – largely thanks to one country: Germany.

The German pavilions   Until Brussels 1910, Germany had approached the world exhibition phenomenon half-heartedly. It had not hosted a large-scale event (though it had wanted the 1900 fair) and time and time again the only great attraction among its official entries was the Krupp company's canon installation. Previous German pavilions were rendered in historical styles and stuffed with ostentatious furniture. And sometimes there was no German presence at all – at Paris 1878, for example. But the German entry for Brussels 1910 more than made up for its history of indifference. Its installation was almost as large as that of the host country, and was equivalent in size to all of the other international pavilions put together. Moreover, the various German pavilions signaled a new direction in European architecture. Influenced by theoretician Paul Mebes and his 1908 work *Um 1800: Architektur und Kunsthandwerk im letzten Jahrhundert ihrer traditionellen Entwicklung*, German architects gave a contemporary interpretation to their classical heritage. With work by Peter Behrens and Bruno Paul, Brussels 1910 became a platform for the new German style.

The exhibition poster reproduced on a brochure for a hairdressing conference held at the fair

Reception area by Paul Thiersch

Ladies Room designed
by Heinrich Vogeler

Director's Room of a
School for Handicrafts
designed by Wilhelm
Thiele

Whereas Paul tended toward the decorative, Behrens pointed the Germans to a union of art and industry. In essence, the German installation was a preview of the famous 1914 Deutscher Werkbund exhibition in Cologne.

The German section was comprised of a number of buildings arranged according to a plan by architect Emanuel von Seidl, who was also responsible for several of the pavilions. Typical of his style, which was influenced by Mebes and by the influential critic Hermann Muthesius, were undulating roofs, taut classical forms, and white plastered walls. Muthesius attended the exhibition and was impressed by the German entries. Behrens, who had recently completed his famous AEG turbine factory in Berlin, was responsible for the German Railway Hall. The structure, with columns of a rudimentary Doric order and a rivet-studded steel I-beam over the entrance, clearly referenced a classical temple building. The framework, a collaboration between Behrens and engineer Hermann Kügler, used a recently patented system of laminated wood beams.

Main entrance to the
German Pavilion, archi-
tect Emanuel von Seidl

Germany's Kultushalle,
architect Bruno Paul,
fountain by Paul
Peterich

Delmenhorster
Linoleum Factory instal-
lation by Peter Behrens

German Pavilion for
Interior and Applied
Arts, architect Bruno
Paul

The Delmenhorster
Linoleum Factory pro-
duced designs for floor
coverings by the archi-
tects Albert Gessner
(above, left), Peter
Behrens (below, left),
and Bruno Paul (above
and below, right)

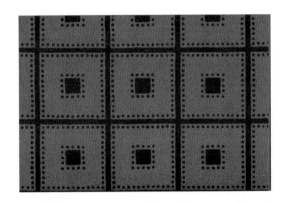

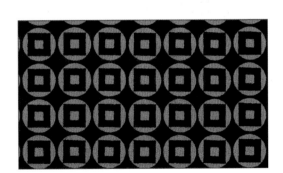

Original design by
WIllem Kromhout for
the Dutch Pavilion
(1908)

Kromhout's revised
design for the Dutch
Pavilion (1909)

Executed design by
Kromhout for the Dutch
Pavilion (1910)

German Railway
Pavilion, architect
Peter Behrens

Palais des Travaux
Feminins (left).
Photograph from one of
the entrances to the site

German interiors The German interiors were of a somber classicism that demonstrated a strong affinity with the work of Karl Friedrich Schinkel. Behrens – who had also executed interiors for the Turin 1902 and Saint Louis 1904 exhibitions – was responsible for the Delmenhorster Linoleum installation. Delmenhorster's flooring products featured striking geometric designs by Behrens, Paul, and Albert Gessner. The interiors of the Kultushalle and the Raumkunst und Kunstgewerbe pavilions were designed by Paul. His well-articulated spaces were divided into geometric forms that, like Behrens' Railway Hall, evoked the architecture of classical temples. The German pavilions also boasted work by such luminaries as Richard Riemerschmid and Paul Thiersch as well as lesser-known designers like Max Heidrich, and Wilhelm Thiele.

Other structures If the burned and rebuilt Grand Palais was seen as *retardataire*, it was not alone. The distinguished architect H. J. P. Berlage derided the Dutch Pavilion – a banal neorenaissance building – as an insult to modern architecture, especially in that the architect, Willem Kromhout, had originally submitted two progressive designs. Berlage, whose own work was exhibited in drawings and photographs at the exhibition, shared Muthesius's high regard for the German installation. Meanwhile, a melange of theme buildings on the Avenue des Nations (an Ardennes hut, an Arabian fortress, a Swiss châlet, a Tuscan villa, a Bavarian farmhouse, and an Indian temple) attracted the general public.

Panama-Pacific International Exposition

San Francisco

Year **1915 (20 March – 4 December)** Location **San Francisco** Surface area **635 acres** Attendance **18,876,438** Participating nations **24** Architectural supervisor **George Kelham** Kleurenschema **Jules Guerin**

The Palace of Fine
Arts, architect
Bernard Maybeck

Plan of the exhibition
site

Seldom has an exhibition endured so many unexpected and tragic setbacks as San Francisco 1915. The motivation for the exhibition was to mark the opening of the Panama Canal and the subsequent development of the Pacific Coast as a center of international commerce. (One of the fair's great attractions would be a 5-acre model of the canal toured from a moving platform.) San Francisco, however, was not the only city that sought to celebrate this event. San Diego also vied for the right to host the fair, and in the end held its own, smaller exhibition in the same year. Competition was the least of San Francisco's problems. In 1906, barely two years after San Francico had begun planning for the event, an earthquake followed by a great fire reduced the city to ashes. San Francisco rebuilt, but as the American economy went into recession, funding for the exhibition evaporated. Finally, World War I erupted, limiting international participation and dashing the "brotherhood-of-man" ideal. Nevertheless, San Francisco managed to host one of the largest and most exceptional of all exhibitions.

Site and main buildings

In purposeful contrast to the stark plaster whiteness of both Chicago 1893 and St. Louis 1904, San Francisco's Panama-Pacific Exposition was a blaze of color. The exposition company imported a designer – Jules Guerin – from New York to create a comprehensive color scheme for the event, the centerpiece of which was a 432-foot tower of colored glass pieces. The overall effect was so successful that the exhibition was dubbed the "Jewel City."

As with so many world exhibitions, the site for the event was situated along a waterfront: the San Francisco Bay, with its expansive views of Sausalito and Golden Gate. A planning committee, led by George Kelham, chose to group the eight main pavilions around an oval plaza, McKim, Mead & White's Court of the Universe. This arrangement was chosen based on the experience of the St. Louis exhibition, where buildings that were too widely spaced allowed wind and rain to trouble visitors. The themes of the eight pavilions, which were linked by connecting walkways with rounded arches, were education, agriculture, mining, food production, the arts, transportation, manufacturing, and industry. Beyond the core buildings was Bernard Maybeck's extraordinary Palace of Fine Arts. Surprisingly, Maybeck was only a draftsman in the office of Willis Polk when he designed the opulent building (Polk was a former pupil of Maybeck's who hired the senior architect when his career slumped). The Palace of Fine Arts was so popular that it was not destroyed after the fair, though it was conceived and constructed as a temporary structure. It gradually withered until 1965, when it was entirely rebuilt – following a protracted funding drive – with permanent materials.

San Francisco after the
1906 earthquake

Overview across the
Court of the Ages with
the Tower of Jewels and
the Arch of the Rising
Sun in the background.
In the foreground is the
Fountain of the Earth

Like the original Fine Arts building, the exhibition's pavilions were constructed with frames of California timber and finished with a layer of plaster and hemp upon which more precious materials (marble and travertine) were painted in imitation. All of the buildings were painted according to Guerin's color scheme (in soft peach, ultramarine, fawn, amber, and verdigris). The landscaping was also coordinated to Guerin's design. The result was a visual *horror vacui* at the heart of which stood Thomas Hastings' Tower of Jewels. Located on the central square, the tower was encrusted with a shimmering layer of fifty thousand Austrian glass fragments in yellow, violet, ruby red, aquamarine, and white. The tower itself was lit by pulsating red lights, symbolically indicating the beating artery of the American continent. The other buildings were also carefully illuminated – under the direction of lighting designer Walter D'Arcy Ryan – to enhance their colors.

World's Fairs

Dutch Pavilion, architect Willem Kromhout

Dome of the Palace of Fine Arts, architect Bernard Maybeck. Between 1965 and 1967 the palace was rebuilt with durable materials

Night illumination of the Tower of Jewels, architect Thomas Hastings of Carrère and Hastings

The Horticulture
Building, demolished
in 1955

Overview of the exhibi-
tion site with the Tower
of Jewels in the back-
ground

The pavilions Twenty-four nations were represented at the Panama-Pacific Exposition, despite the raging world war. Four of the pavilions – from France, Greece, Italy, and Norway – were transported from Europe to the site on the USS *Jason*, and opened nearly four months late. The French Pavilion, a copy of the Hôtel de Salm in Paris, served as a tribute to French action in the trenches and was hailed by flocking exhibition crowds. One of the most successful foreign entries was the Dutch Pavilion, designed by Willem Kromhout. Influenced by early Christian and Byzantine architecture, it radiated an almost sacred aura, with colors that diverged from the exhibition's official program. As at St. Louis, the majority of the American buildings were in the predominant classical style. The Pennsylvania State Pavilion, however, was a reproduction of Independence Hall, and the Oregon entry was an imitation Parthenon with trees for columns.

San Diego Despite its limited site (194 acres compared to San Francisco's 635) and modest ambitions, the Panama-California Exposition was also a success, with attendance reaching nearly four million. It remained open for 1916, allowing many of the foreign pavilions to be transported south after the close of the San Francisco fair. The San Diego exhibition would also have a lasting influence on the American landscape: in contrast to the classical forms of the San Francisco exhibition, the Panama-California fair featured Spanish Colonial architecture, and was highly influential in the dissemination of that style throughout the American West.

Court of the Universe, architects McKim, Mead & White. In the background is the Arch of the Setting Sun, in the foreground, the fountains of *Day* and *Night*

Colonnade of the Palace of Fine Arts

Court of the Four
Seasons, architect
Henry Bacon. The *Ceres*
Fountain is a design by
Evelyn Beatrice
Longman

The sad fate of many of
the exhibition buildings
was demolition

Exposition Internationale des Arts Décoratifs et Industriels Modernes

Paris

12.- PARIS. Exposition des Arts Décoratifs
Pont Alexandre-III - Rue des Boutiques (composée par Maurice Dufrêne)

The reinforced concrete Pavillon du Tourisme, architect Robert Mallet-Stevens

The Pont Alexandre III with the Rue des Boutiques, designed by Maurice Dufrêne

Year **1925 (April – October)** Location **Paris (Esplanade des Invalides, Avenue Alexandre III)** Surface area **57 acres** Participating nations **18** Attendance **5,852,783** Architect and supervisor **Charles Plumet** Novelties **The Machine for Living, plywood furniture**

The Exposition Internationale des Arts Décoratifs et Industriels Modernes remains among the most notable of twentieth-century fairs, though it was a thematic rather than a universal exhibition. The fair signaled the ascendance of art deco, the new style that was flourishing internationally, especially in the applied arts. Though Paris 1925 did not mark the first appearance of art deco, as is sometimes suggested, it did serve to both validate the style and give it a broader audience. For the occasion, art deco was officially promoted by the French minister for fine arts, and the Pont Alexandre III was swathed with overblown art deco ornament. The cubistic forms of the French pavilions, in particular, were widely acclaimed at the time. This reception was particularly notable considering that the homeland of the École des Beaux Arts was not always receptive to new trends, as demonstrated by its classical government buildings.

Europe was so decimated by World War I that it was 1925 before a truly international exhibition could be put together (the vast British Empire Exhibition of 1924 –1925 was largely restricted to the Commonwealth). Even still, it was smaller in scale than previous Parisian exhibitions: only the Esplanade des Invalides and Avenue Alexandre III were used. And despite the characteristic theme of international peace and goodwill, Weimar Germany was not invited.

New voices The initial impetus for the exhibition was born in 1906, when a youthful group that had played a subordinate role at the Paris 1900 event organized an exhibition of modern French art. Their goal was to reinstate Paris as the capital of progressive thinking in the arts, a position they felt it had lost. Reacting against Beaux-Arts classicism, this younger generation emphatically renounced any discrete formal vocabulary. It is therefore somewhat ironic that when the exhibition they had called for was finally held, art deco was itself on the road to becoming the established order.

Cubistic garden by
Robert Mallet Stevens.
The women's outfits
were designed by Sonia
Delaunay

Plan of the exhibition
site

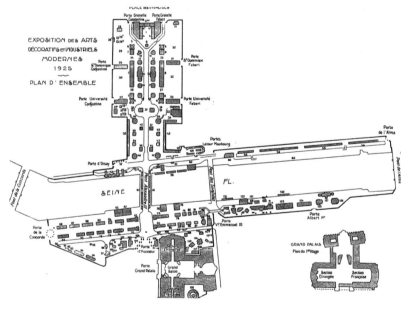

Exposition des Arts Décoratifs

VUE GÉNÉRALE

Exposition des Arts Décoratifs

LE PAVILLON PRIMAVERA DU PRINTEMPS

Overview of the exhibition site

Le Pavillon Primavera du Printemps, architect Henri Sauvage

The standard bearer of the new generation of architects was Le Corbusier, who ardently railed against the purely decorative nature of art deco. Those in Le Corbusier's camp, as might be expected, were thus not received with open arms in Paris. This situation was exacerbated by the presentation of Le Corbusier's "Plan voisin" at the fair. This scheme called for the leveling of much of Paris, which would then be replaced with a series of towers set in landscaped parks. Less specifically, though modernism and cubism were the inspirations for art deco, their internationalism offended many French citizens. This prejudice explains why the paintings of Fernand Léger and Robert Delaunay were removed from the Ambassade Française show at the fair, and why the exhibition's board of directors had a 20-foot fence erected around Le Corbusier's Pavillon de l'Esprit Nouveau (only removed after the intercession of the minister of fine arts). Though the exhibition was ostensibly held to present modern design, neither work in the De Stijl nor the Bauhaus idioms was represented. More to the taste of the general public were artists such as Louis Suë, André Mare, and Jacques-Emile Ruhlmann, whose luxurious works in expensive materials recalled the golden age of French design. A noteworthy modern counterpoint to their work was Robert Mallet-Stevens's reinforced concrete design for the Pavillon du Tourisme.

Entrance and hall of the
Pavillon du Tourisme

Pavillon de l'Esprit
Nouveau, architect Le
Corbusier. The sculp-
ture in the foreground
is by Jacques Lipschitz

PAVILLON U.R.S.S.
PARIS 1925

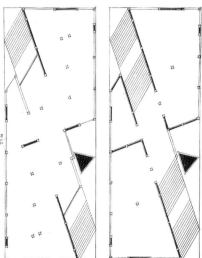

Design for the Soviet
Pavilion by Konstantin
Melnikov

Plan of the Soviet
Pavilion

The Czechoslovakian
Pavilion, architect
Joseph Gocár, sculpture
by Stursa

Monumental Entrance
by Pierre Patout

Exposition des
Arts Décoratifs
Pavillon Tchéco-Slovaque

Exposition des Arts Décoratifs

Patout. Arch.   Porte de la Concorde

Pavilions Le Corbusier's Pavillon de l'Esprit Nouveau, made financially possible by the industrialist Gabriel Voisin, was actually a demonstration living unit from a block of dwellings of the future. In rudimentary form, it demonstrated Le Corbusier's "Five Points" for a new architecture: *pilotis* (stilts), roof terraces, ribbon windows, a free plan, and a free façade. Like the Pavillon du Tourisme, it was of reinforced concrete. The interior contained modular cabinets, Thonet chairs, and tubular furniture (Corbusier mechanistically referred to these accoutrements as *"l'équipement de la maison"*). Cubist paintings and other unusual items (including a tree that was incorporated into the building) served as adornment. The whole was intended as what the architect famously described as a *"machine à habiter"* (machine for living), a rejection of decorative art and proof that industrialized and standardized design could produce a beautiful and functional environment.

Other noteworthy pavilions not in the art deco style were produced by foreign delegations. The Soviet Union, represented for the first time at a world exhibition, had commissioned the radical architect Konstantin Melnikov to design its pavilion. Melnikov's dynamic building blurred boundaries between inner and outer spaces, it's wall plane constantly shifting in a sea of red paint. Austria was represented by Joseph Hoffmann, who produced an almost postmodern design with an interior by Josef Frank and a conservatory by Peter Behrens. Ironically, it was the totalitarian regimes that gave the avant garde its best opportunities for display, though the same regimes would opt for reactionary and pompous neo-classicism in coming decades.

Of the French pavilions, the most interesting were the Théâtre de l'Exposition by Auguste Perret (with A. Grenet) and the Pavillon Rhône-Loire by Tony Garnier. Perret's exquisite theater, regarded as an art deco trailblazer, was pulled down a few months after it was built. Henri Sauvage designed a pavilion for the Printemps department store, and Mallet-Stevens a garden of reinforced concrete trees. In fact, all the leading exponents of French architecture were represented.

The Austrian Pavilion conservatory, architect Peter Behrens

The Austrian Pavilion, architect Josef Hoffmann

The Dutch Pavilion,
architect Jan Frederiks
Staal. Interior
Hendricus Theodorus
Wijdeveld

The Belgian Pavilion,
architect Victor Horta

Exposition des Arts Décoratifs
PAVILLON DE BELGIQUE
HORTA. Arch.

Exposición General d'España

Exposición Internacional de Barcelona Barcelona

Exposición Ibero-Americana   Seville

An impression of the exhibition's much-lauded light show seen from the Avenida Reina Maria Cristina with the Palau Nacional in the background

Bird's-eye view of the exhibition site

Year **1929–30 (May – January)**   Location **Barcelona (Parque de Montjuïc – Plaza de España)** Surface area **291.5 acres**

Location **Seville**   Surface area **170.5 acres**   Head of state **Miguel Primo de Rivera (military dictatorship)** Regent **Alfonso XIII**

Barcelona 1929 remains famous for the German Pavilion – the "Barcelona Pavilion" – designed by Ludwig Mies van der Rohe. The other exhibition buildings have faded from memory despite the fact that the most important ones still exist, a rarity given the normally temporary nature of fair construction. (Ironically, the German Pavilion mysteriously vanished while being shipped back to Germany after the exhibition.) In 1929, however, visitors were more impressed by the overall metropolitan allure of the site and its monumental buildings. It was almost a quarter of a century before the German Pavilion was recognized as one of the great signature buildings in the history of Western architecture.

Themes The fair's organizers originally intended to hold the exhibition in 1917; the theme was to be "Electricity." But the worldwide political situation combined with internal Spanish instability to force the twelve-year delay. Only after the dictatorial Catalan Primo de Rivera came to power did the exhibition take on concrete form. Two sites were named: Barcelona and Seville. In Barcelona, the principal themes were to be "Industry," "Spanish Art," and "Sports." Seville, one of the country's most important port cities, was to exhibit Spain's colonial wealth.

A matter of style The fact that its pavilion was not lauded by contemporary architectural critics must have been hard on the German delegation. Present at a world exhibition for the first time since the war, they had spared no expense and had deliberately chosen a progressive architect capable of expressing the democratic ideals of the Weimar Republic. With its open plan, reflecting pools, carefully placed sculpture, onyx walls, and eponymous leather chairs, the German Pavilion is today considered the apogee of ethereal elegance. At the fair, it was situated along the route to the immensely popular Spanish Village. It was also one of only a handful of modern structures (the Yugoslavian Pavilion was another), and thus could hardly have been overlooked by visitors. So why did it not receive the attention it so deserved?

The reasons may be found within the architectural context of the exhibition. As time has passed, the fair's architecture has been increasingly depicted as a confused jumble of styles. In fact, there were several movements waging stylistic war on the Barcelona site. In addition to art deco, imported from Paris, there was Catalan modernism (exemplified by the work of Antoni Gaudí) and noucentisme (a more classically oriented rejoinder to modernism). Judged by the volume of structures constructed, noucentisme, with its symmetrical forms and baroque plans, was the victor.

Perhaps the pomp and circumstance of the predominant architecture of the fair – not to mention its spectacular illumination – diverted attention from the refined German Pavilion. In any case, it was not the first time that an extraordinary work of exhibition architecture was not immediately recognized as such: both the Eiffel Tower (1889) and Le Corbusier's Esprit Nouveau Pavilion (1929) were brutally received in Paris.

Old-Age Pension Fund Pavilion

The Yugoslavian
Pavilion

The Italian Pavilion

The German Pavilion,
architect Mies van der
Rohe

Photograph of the
nightly light show seen
from the Avenida Reina
Maria Cristina, with the
Palau Nacional in the
background

The rear of the Palau
Nacional, architects
Enric Càta i Càta, Pedro
Cendoya i Oscoz, and
Pere Domènech i Roura

Of far more interest to
visitors than the inter-
national pavilions was
the Pueblo Espanol, a
Spanish village with
indigenous architecture
from various periods
and regions. Architects
Francesco Foluera and
Ramon Reventos

Main Building of the
Seville exhibition

The Palau Nacional,
now a museum of
Catalan art. Restoration
1985 – 1992 by Gae
Aulenti and Enric
Steegmann

The Palace of Graphic
Arts, now the City
Archeological Museum.
architects Pelagi
Martinez i Paricio,
Raimon Dural Reynals.
Restauration 1984 – 1989
by José Llinàs

The Palace of Textile
Art

Site and buildings At the foot of the Montjuïc, the fair entrance was fronted by two imposing Venetian towers dedicated to Christopher Columbus. A direct route led to the waterworks of the Palau Nacional (National Palace), which, like many of the fair's buildings, were illuminated in various colors. Great care was taken with the lighting. The site itself was designed by the landscape engineer Jean Forestier with the assistance of architect Nicolas Rubio Tuduri, who also designed several hotels built in anticipation of the many visitors the fair expected to draw. Together, the two men were also responsible for the Greek Theater. Puig i Cadafalch designed two identical palaces for Alfonso XIII and Victoria Eugenia. The Palau Nacional (now a museum of Catalan art) was designed by Enric Catà i Catà, Pedro Cendoya i Oscoz and Pere Domènech i Roura, and was located at the end of the exhibition's central thoroughfare. Other still extant buildings include Casa de la Prensa (now a police station) by Pere Domènech, the Hall of Agriculture (a theater) by Mayol Ferrer and Ribas, and the Hall of Graphic Arts (the City Archeological Museum) by Pelagi Martínez Paricio, and Ramon Dural Reynals. To accommodate sports – not normally associated with world's fairs – a municipal stadium was designed by Domènech i Roura. The Spanish Village was designed by Francesco Foluera and Ramon Reventos.

Most of these buildings were in the noucentisme style, with forms borrowed from both the Spanish Renaissance and the Italian Renaissance – the latter because the Italian city-state was seen as an ideal model by many Catalan architects. Josep Goday i Casals's design for the Pabellon de la Ciudad de Barcelona, for example, was inspired by the Florentine works of Brunelleschi.

153

Exposition International, Colonial, Maritime, et d'Art Flemmand Antwerp

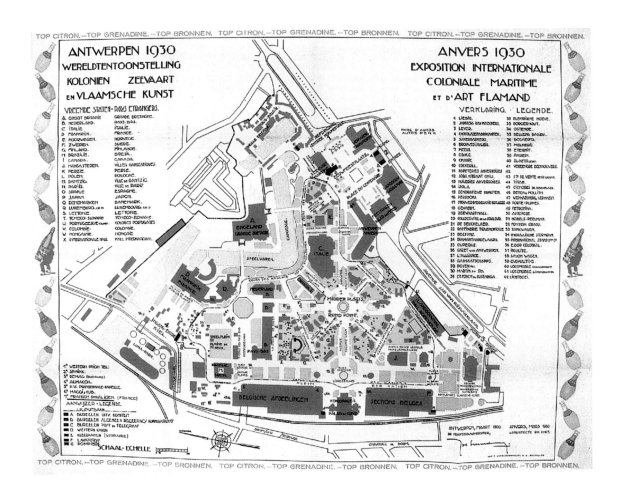

The Antwerp City Pavilion, architect Emiel Van Averbeeke

Plan of the exhibition site

Year **1930 (26 April – 4 November)** Location **Antwerp** Surface area **170.5 acres** Attendance **5.2 million** Participating nations **21** Architect and supervisor **Joseph Smolderen** Head of state and High Patron of the Exhibtion **King Albert**

The Dutch Pavilion,
architect Hendricus
Theodorus Wijdeveld

Interior of the Dutch
Pavilion

Main Entrance to the
exhibition site

Like the Paris event of 1925, Antwerp's third international exhibition was seriously delayed by World War I. The decision to hold the event in Belgium actually coincided with the outbreak of the war, and, complicating matters, after the war it remained unresolved which Belgian city would host it. Although private investors had secured the exhibition for Belgium – unlike most countries, exhibitions in Belgium were organized in the private sector – the venue was chosen by the government. In 1926 the Belgian legislature passed the Salomon Ruling, stipulating that Brussels would hold a large world exhibition (in 1935) and that Antwerp and Liège would host a combined event in 1930, with the main themes divided between the two cities. The opening of the Antwerp exhibition coincided with the opening of a new lock of the Scheldt River, but its true *raison d'être* was the centennial commemoration of the Belgian secession from the Netherlands.

Site Antwerp had hoped for considerably more than the thematic colonial exhibition that it was assigned. To make up for the perceived indignity, the fair's organizers sought to include every conceivable export product in the fair. In a sense this was appropriate: the great port city of the Scheldt had always been a trading town.

Antwerp's Exposition Universelle of 1885 had taken place on Het Zuid, a vacant urban space that had since been developed. The 1930 site was upriver, held along the Antwerp Zuid to Mechelen rail line and the Van Rijswijcklaan. The site plan, which included a nearby ancient rampart, had already been completed in 1926 by Emiel Van Averbeeke, but it was executed and modified by Jos Smolderen. Avenues radiated from central points connected by a fragmented network of smaller roads. Though it had been originally intended that large pavilions would be situated on the outer edges with the smaller pavilions on the interior, in the end smaller structures were spread haphazardly over the site. This made for a variegated fair experience, though it disrupted the clarity of Van Averbeeke's plan.

In addition to those from Belgium, the largest pavilions were from England, France, and Italy. The Belgian pavilions were grouped around the beyond the Main Entrance, a triumphal arch honoring independent Belgium and the first three Belgian monarchs (who appeared in equestrian statues under the arch's three vaults). The archway itself, executed by Smolderen from a designed by Van Averbeeke, was constructed of plaster and wood, as were most of the fair's buildings. Sited on the exhibition periphery was an amusement park and Old Belgium, a picturesque village with houses of various regional and historical styles.

Architecture While art deco and other highly ornamental styles had dominated previous fairs, the buildings at Antwerp were much more reserved. Whether due to recession or the rising influence of modernism, the fact was that decorative embellishment was disappearing from architecture. What remained were blocky and severe volumes. A good example was Van Averbeeke's Antwerp Pavilion, the wings of which were devoid of ornament. The German installations – actually from the cities of Hamburg, Lübeck, and Bremen – were in a similarly plain style. Germany had not sent official national-level representation due to its troubled financial situation. There were also pavilions designed in a restrained classical style, including the British building by Edwin Lutyens, which radiated the might of a colonial super-power (echoed by the pavilion's display on the British race). The installation was not well received. Parisian, Portuguese, and Dutch entries were in the art deco style. Along with the European nations, former colonies were represented by independent pavilions. As on previous occasions, Brazil stood out with a luxuriously furnished art deco building. Two buildings were intended for posterity: Christus Koning church, in which Flemish art was exhibited, and a second pavilion for fine art that was later converted to a school. Both were designed by Van Averbeeke.

Modernism was noticeably absent from the exhibition. Russia, represented in 1925 with a building by Konstantin Melnikov, failed to make an appearance, while those countries where modernist thinking supposedly thrived exhibited in more decorative styles. In an effort to create a friendly exhibition atmosphere, various follies and gimmicky symbolic structures were placed prominently on the grounds. In 1930, frivolity and classicism still went hand in hand. Five years later, at the Brussels exhibition of 1935, this relationship began to dissolve. By the 1937 Paris fair it had disappeared altogether.

The Italian Pavilion

The English Pavilion, architect Edwin Lutyens

The Luna Park amuse-
ment zone under con-
struction

Official exhibition
poster (in Spanish),
design by Marfurt

The Temple of Flemish
Art, later the Christus
Koningkerk (church),
architect Emiel Van
Averbeeke

The Brazilian Pavilion

A Century of Progress Exposition Chicago

The Chrysler Building, architects Holabird and Root

View of Northerly Island from the Sky Ride. A "Rocket Car" approaches on the tramway

Year **1933 (27 May – 12 November); 1934 (25 May – 31 October)** Location **Chicago (Lakefront, Northerly Island)** Attendance **48,769,227** Surface area **426 acres** President **Rufus C. Dawes** Chairman, Architectural Commission **Harvey Wiley Corbett** Chief of Design **Louis Skidmore** Color Director **Joseph Urban**

The initial idea for an exhibition to celebrate the centennial of Chicago was first expressed in 1923 and adopted by the city in 1926. An exhibition commission was soon formed with Rufus C. Dawes as president and Daniel H. Burnham Jr. as secretary. Burnham's father, of course, had been the chief of construction at the World's Columbian Exposition of 1893 (another of his sons, Hubert Burnham, served on the second fair's architectural committee). The Columbian Exposition established the legitimacy of both host city and nation as industrial and cultural powers. Forty years later, their roles were no longer in question; the Century of Progress Exposition could look back on one hundred years of industrial development, and, more importantly, look forward to a future of technological advancement. In the midst of the Depression, the sense of optimism that permeated the fair was a crucial element of its success. Visitors flocked to the exhibition, which was backed financially by several of Chicago's wealthiest citizens, providing a boost for both the local economy and the city's morale. For these reasons, and at the behest of President Franklin Delano Roosevelt, the exhibition remained open for a second year, 1934.

The site Like the Columbian Exposition, the Century of Progress fair was held along the Chicago lakefront (a three mile stretch supplemented by the artificial Northerly Island). And also like the earlier fair, a commission of Beaux-Arts trained architects from the East Coast directed design. The commission was chaired by Harvey Wiley Corbett – a New Yorker whose fantastic visions of cities of the future suited him well for the job – and was comprised of Raymond Hood, Ralph Walker, Paul Philippe Cret, and Arthur Brown. Chicagoans John A. Holabird, Edward H. Bennett, and Hubert Burnham were later added. The commission chose Louis Skidmore as chief of design, and proceeded to divide up the site between themselves, with each architect responsible for the design of his own section. The buildings that resulted were generally of a stripped-down but high-tech modernestyle. Theatrical designer Joseph Urban was brought in from New York as color director, and he proceeded to paint the entire fair in bright colors. If the Columbian Exposition was a "White City," the Century of Progress was anything but. Like that earlier fair, however, a variety of theme and

An artists impression of the exhibition with the towers of the Sky RIde in the center

The United States Building, architect Edward H. Bennett

The Travel and Transport Building, architects John A. Holabird, Edward H. Bennett, and Hubert Burnham

amusement installations were constructed on an area known as the Midway. Two of the most popular of these attractions were the Belgian Village and the Streets of Cairo. Reproductions of the log cabins in which Abraham Lincoln was born and raised also proved popular. The arts played an important role in the exhibition, with many otherwise bare walls decorated by murals and relief work. Notable was Thomas Hart Benton's 250-foot mural depicting the history of Indiana, located in the Court of the States. Contemporary art was exhibited along with the works of old masters: Grant Wood's American Gothic, Marcel Duchamp's Nude Descending a Staircase, and Rembrandt's Aristotle with the Bust of Homer were all on display.

The Sky Ride   The architectural commission originally intended to mark the site with a giant tower, but with the onset of the Depression this became financially unfeasible. Its replacement was the Sky Ride, an elevated tram system designed by Joshua d'Esposito that ran between two 628-foot towers placed 2,000 feet apart (one stanchion on the mainland, the other on Northerly Island). Streamlined gondolas – known as "rocket cars" – carried fairgoers back and forth at the 210-foot level, providing spectacular views of the fair site and the city beyond.

Architecture A series of impressive modern buildings littered the site. Among the most interesting was Holabird, Bennett, and Burnham's Travel and Transportation Building, a dome – 205 feet in diameter – suspended by steel cables strung from 150-foot towers surrounding the structure. Bennett's United States Building featured three triangular towers symbolizing the branches of American government. Raymond Hood's semicircular Electricity Building, situated on Northerly Island, was accessible by boat, and Albert Kahn's gigantic General Motors Building featured an entire Chevrolet production line (the fair supposedly featured the "process" of progress, not its products). Of the foreign pavilions, Adalberto Libera's Italian entry, with its giant stylized fasces stands out. The structure was based on his design for the Exhibition of the Tenth Anniversary of the Fascist Revolution, which would be reprised yet again at the Brussels 1935 fair.

One of the more popular attractions at the fair was the Home and Industrial Arts Exhibit, which featured a variety of model low-cost, single-family homes designed with prefabricated, standardized parts. All were modern in style. The most interesting of these were a pair of buildings designed by the Chicago firm Keck & Keck. The first, the House of Tomorrow, was a three level octagonal structure slung from a central utility core, much like R. Buckminster Fuller's Dymaxion House. The second, the Crystal House (installed for the 1934 season), was a boxy three story structure with walls of glass panels. These panels were supported by a series of steel trusses that framed the small building. Fuller's Dymaxion Car was parked in its covered driveway.

In addition to the picturesque Belgian Village and the Streets of Cairo, "anthropological" exhibitions like "Darkest Africa" drew large crowds. Not surprisingly, African-American participation in the exhibition was limited, though the fair corporation had adopted a nondiscriminatory hiring policy. Nevertheless, the exhibition, especially at the administrative levels, was a lily-white affair.

An artists rendering captures the saturated color of the event

The Italian Pavilion, architects Adalberto Libera and Mario de Renzi

The House of Tomorrow, architects Keck & Keck

The General Motors Building, architect Albert Kahn

Exposition Universelle et Internationale de Bruxelles Bruxelles

PLAN DE L'EXPOSITION

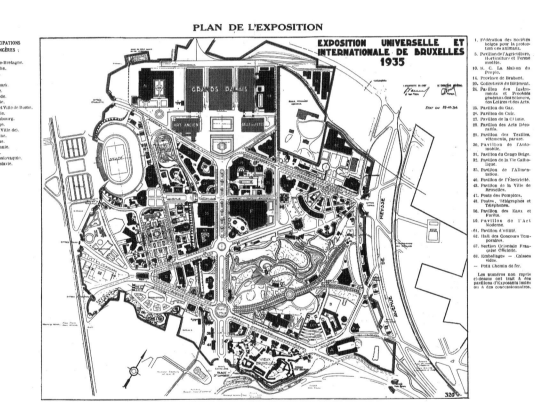

EXPOSITION UNIVERSELLE ET INTERNATIONALE DE BRUXELLES 1935

PARTICIPATIONS ÉTRANGÈRES :

A.   Grande-Bretagne.
Au. Autriche.
B.   Brésil.
C.   Chili.
D   Danemark.
F.   France.
H.   Hollande.
Hon. Hongrie.
I.   Italie et Ville de Rome.
Let. Lettonie.
L.   Luxembourg.
N.   Norvège.
P.   Paris (Ville de).
Pal. Palestine.
Pol. Pologne.
R.   Roumanie.
Su. Suède.
Tch. Tchécoslovaquie.
Y.   Yougoslavie.

1. Fédération des Sociétés belges pour la protection des animaux.
5. Pavillon de l'Agriculture, Horticulture et Ferme modèle.
10. S. C. La Maison du Peuple.
14. Province de Brabant.
20. Collectivité du Bâtiment.
24. Pavillon des Instruments et Procédés généraux des Sciences, des Lettres et des Arts.
25. Pavillon du Gaz.
26. Pavillon du Cuir.
27. Pavillon de la Chimie.
28. Pavillon des Arts Décoratifs.
29. Pavillon des Textiles, vêtements, parure.
30. Pavillon de l'Automobile.
31. Pavillon du Congo Belge.
32. Pavillon de la Vie Catholique.
35. Pavillon de l'Alimentation.
40. Pavillon de l'Électricité.
44. Pavillon de la Ville de Bruxelles.
47. Poste des Pompiers.
48. Postes, Télégraphes et Téléphones.
56. Pavillon des Eaux et Forêts.
59. Pavillon de l'Art Moderne.
61. Pavillon d'utilité.
62. Hall des Concours Temporaires.
67. Section Coloniale Française Officielle.
68. Emballages — Caisses vides.
— Petit Chemin de fer.

Les numéros non repris ci-dessus ont trait à des pavillons d'Exposants isolés ou à des concessionnaires.

A watercolor of the Dutch Pavilion by V. de Groux. Architect D. Roosenburg

Plan of the exhibition site

Year **1935 (27 April – 35 November)** Location **Brussels Osseghem** Surface area **370.6 acres** Attendance **20 million** Participating nations **24** Head of State **Léopold III** Chief architect **Joseph van Neck** Chief engineer **Paul Célis**

The Brussels exhibition of 1935 has been largely forgotten, eclipsed by the more pompous architectural fury of the exhibition that followed it two years later in Paris. In his otherwise comprehensive book *The Great Exhibitions*, John Allwood devotes all of one paragraph to it, and not a word on the architecture. Wolfgang Friebe, in *Buildings of the World Exhibitions*, omits the year 1935 altogether. This silence is unjustified. From an architectural viewpoint, Brussels 1935 witnessed the aftermath of art deco and the growing presences of two styles divergent in both their formal vocabularies and their ideological underpinnings: monumental classicism and modernism.

The German Pavilion

With his competition design for the German Pavilion, Mies van der Rohe attempted to navigate the difficult space between these two theoretically opposed styles. This was the same architect whose pavilion for Barcelona 1929 had symbolized the peacefulness and democratic values of the Weimar Republic. Barely five years later, Mies, by invitation, entered the competition for the Brussels pavilion. Sponsored by Joseph Goebbels' Nazi Ministry of Propaganda, the brief called for a hall of honor and four exhibition spaces that would present Hitler's deluded ideas. It also demanded that the pavilion be an imposing expression of military power and heroism. Modernism in Germany stood on the eve of condemnation, but at the time of the competition it had not yet been declared taboo. Mies's design borrowed elements from his Barcelona pavilion, but the whole was larger, more monumental, and more spiritual (note the "altar" in the hall of honor). Fundamentally, it stood directly opposed to the founding ideals of modernism. In the end, Mies did not win the competition but was commissioned for the interior. This was abandoned due to financial difficulties between Belgium and Germany, whereby the latter felt obliged not to send any delegation at all.

Site

In contrast to the jumbled organization of Antwerp 1930, for the Brussels 1935 event the various pavilions were evenly spread over the exhibition terrain, fully exploiting the undulating Osseghem site. Several axial avenues – one ending on a square with the permanent Grote Paleis (Grand Palais) – segmented the site, carving areas for Old Brussels village, a park, the agriculture section, and the various entertainment spaces. A stadium was also incorporated into the exhibition site and lay in an area not defined by any grand architectural gesture but by more subtle detailing. The overall exhibition area – more than 370 acres – was remarkably well designed.

The pavilions

The main Belgian pavilions displayed a blend of art deco, modernist, and classical forms. Worthy of individual mention is Joseph van Neck's Grote Paleis. The 128-foot building had a 292-foot concrete span that was exhaustively tested for stress before the exhibition. The Electricity Pavilion by Jean Jules Eggricx displayed an electrically driven model farmhouse. Also of note was the Malfait-designed art deco pavilion for the city of Brussels, its 164-foot tower a tribute to the Brussels Belfort, a civic symbol of freedom. One of the most curious structures at the exhibition was the Catholic Living Pavilion, a bizarre, space-age assemblage with an exterior of domes, obelisks, and brass walls, (but a stark, modernist interior). The architect, Henry Lacoste, was also responsible for the Pavilion of Decorative Art and the Greek Pavilion.

Brazilian Pavilion,
architect Barrez

Brussels City Pavilion,
architect Malfait

L'EXPOSITION UNIVERSELLE ET INTERNATIONALE DE BRUXELLES

Superficie totale de l'Exposition : 140 Hectares. — Parc Forestier : 17 Hectares. — Grands Palais : 45.000 mètres carrés.
Stade des Sports de 90.000 places. — Puissance électrique : 20.000 kilowatts. — Plus de 140 Palais et Pavillons.

AVRIL 1935 NOVEMBRE

PARTICIPATIONS ETRANGÈRES

DIRECTION GÉNÉRAL
51, AVENUE DES ARTS
BRUXELLES

Albanie, Allemagne, Autriche, Brésil, Chili, Danemark, France, Grande-Bretagne, Hollande, Hongrie, Italie, Lettonie,
Luxembourg, Norvège, Palestine, Pologne, Roumanie, Suède, Suisse, Tchécoslovaquie, Yougoslavie, etc.

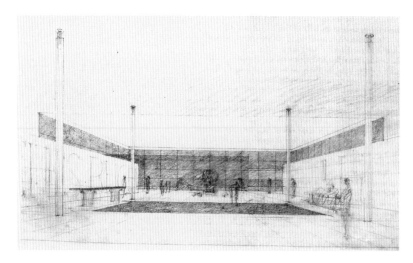

Bird's-eye view of the
exhibition site

Design for the German
Pavilion, court of honor.
Architect, Mies van der
Rohe

The exhibition logo

Luxembourg Pavilion,
architect Trauss & Wolff

Czechoslovakian
Pavilion, architect
Anthonie Heytum

One of the largest foreign entries (over 6 acres with a 164-foot tower) was from fascist Italy. The design, by Adalberto Libera with Mario de Renzi, was essentially a modified version of their 1932 building for the Exhibition of the Tenth Anniversary of the Fascist Revolution in Rome (Mussolini himself had requested that it be used as the pavilion's model). Revised, the façade boasted four giant, stylized fasces applied to a white rectangular block portico punched with a grid of tiny windows. On the interior was a didactic installation on the development of fascism.

The advance of modernism
If modernism was not the predominant style at the exhibition, its exponents were well represented. There were modernist buildings from many private firms and nations, including England, Belgium, Finland, Switzerland, and Norway. This was a departure from the previous fair, Antwerp 1930. In the following exhibition, Paris 1937, monumental classicism would dominate.

The Grote Paleis, architect Joseph van Neck

The Italian Pavilion, architects Adalberto Libera and Mario De Renzi

Advertisement for a
building material exhib-
ited at the British
Pavilion

The Eeuwfeestlaan with
the Grote Paleis in the
background

GEBRUIKT VOOR HET BUITENWERK VAN HET

ENGELSE PAVILJOEN

OP DE WERELDTENTOONSTELLING BRUSSEL 1935

"CULLAMIX"
Bel. Pat. No. 393192

SCRAPED
FINISH
UITGEKRABDE
AFWERKING

Paris City Pavilion,
architect Léon Azéma

Model of the Publicity
Pavilion, architect
Louis H. de Koninck

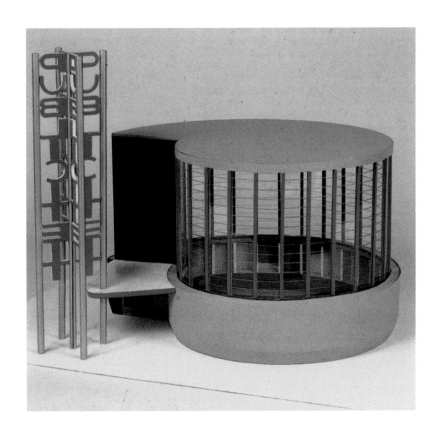

Detail of the Italian
Demonstration Tower

The Swiss Pavilion,
architects Kellermüller
and Hofmann

Catholic Life Pavilion,
architect Henry Lacoste

Exposition Internationale des Arts et des Techniques appliqués à la Vie Moderne

Paris

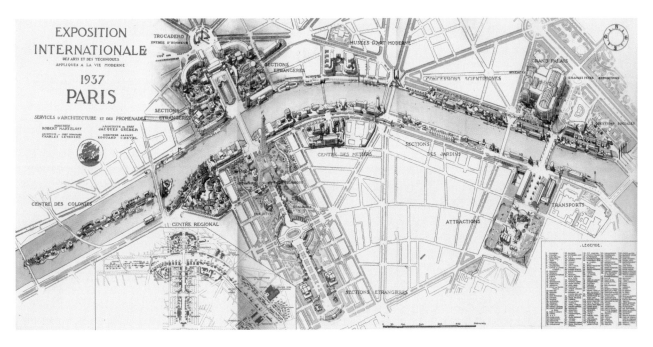

Impression of the 1937 world exhibition by Albert Brenet

Map of the exhibition

Year **1937 (25 May – 25 November)** Location **Paris (Champ de Mars, Trocadéro, banks of the Seine, Esplanade des Invalides)** Surface area **250 acres** Attendance **34 million** Participating nations **44** Chief Architect **Jacques Gréber** Novelties **Plastics, robots** Theme **The art and practice of modern life**

The 1937 world exhibition took place while Spain was being ravaged by civil war, Italy and Germany were redrawing the world map, and Stalin was busily decimating the population of the Soviet Union. These countries were all emphatically present at the exhibition, represented by pompous, intentionally intimidating pavilions. Nevertheless, an atmosphere of progressive optimism somehow remained alive. This feeling was expressed by Jacques Gréber, the French *architect-en-chef*, who glanced at the Monument de la Paix, designed for the exhibition, sighed, and with little apparent foresight stated that it was a symbol of the dawning of good times to come.

The site With forty-four participating countries and thirty-four million visitors, the Paris exhibition was one of the largest ever held. As with the earlier Parisian exhibition of 1889, the site was centered around the Champs de Mars and the Trocadéro. But, as in the Paris fair of 1900, the Esplanade des Invalides and Grand Palais were also incorporated into the event, with the Seine waterfront linking the two zones. The area around the Grand Palais was designated for sciences, social issues, trade, and industry – as well as for parties. Also on the right bank was the newly completed Museum of Modern Art. The old Palais de Trocadéro, built for the 1878 exhibition, was taken down and replaced with the Palais de Chaillot, which still stands today.

The Finnish Pavilion,
architect Alvar Aalto

The demolition of the
old Trocadéro

The Italian Pavilion,
architect Marcello
Piacentini and Cesare
Valle

The Radio Pavilion,
architect Mathon,
Chollet & Sors

EXPOSITION INTERNATIONALE ARTS et TECHNIQUES
PARIS 1937 CENTRE RÉGIONAL

PROVINCES FRANÇAISES

The Belgian Pavilion,
architects Henry van de
Velde, Jean Jules
Eggericx and Raphaël
Verwilghen. Watercolor
by Albert Brenet

The Russian Pavilion,
architect Boris Iofan.
The monumental sculp-
ture on top is by Vera
Mukhina. Other sculp-
tures are by Iosef
Moiseyevich Chaikov

Postcard of the French
regional pavilions

The new Trocadéro seen
from the Eiffel Tower,
architects Carlu,
Boileau, and Azéma.
In the foreground are
the Soviet (left) and
German (right) pavil-
ions

The German pavilion,
architect Albert Speer

The famous Trocadéro fountains were created for the 1937 exhibition, and around these were grouped most of the foreign pavilions. The remainder were sited on the sparsely occupied Champs de Mars. The Ile St. Germain was designated for the French colonies. A picturesque village of pavilions from France's provinces sat on the left bank. In total, there were some 190 large and small buildings. There was not, however, one central hall where the world's production could be displayed, nor were there any great structures of steel and glass of the type that had so defined earlier Parisian fairs.

A battle of style

Though the exhibition was intended to bring the peoples of all nations closer together, the 1937 event was one of unvarnished nationalism. This was expressed in a series of shamelessly bombastic, classically-inspired buildings. Directly facing each other across the Champ de Mars were the pavilions of Nazi Germany (designed by Hitler favorite Albert Speer) and the Soviet Union (by Boris Iofan). The two nations might have been ideologically opposed, but both chose to represent themselves with similarly monumental structures. The German and Soviet pavilions competed with those of Italy (Marcello Piacentini and Cesare Valle), France, and a host of other nations in efforts to achieve the greatest monumentality. This was accomplished through the use of a strictly hierarchical classical vocabulary virtually devoid of ornamentation.

Interior of the Spanish Pavilion, architects Josep Lluis Sert and Josep Lacasa.

Exterior of the Spanish Pavilion

The tower of the
German Pavilion

Museum of Modern Art, architects Dondel, Aubert, Viard and Dastugue

The footbridge at the Porte de l'Alma, architect Marc Solorateff

Festive lighting of the Eiffel Tower and the international pavilions on the bank of the Seine

The modified interior of
the Grand Palais, archi-
tects Madeline, Lebout,
and Madelain

The Electricity Pavilion,
architect Robert Mallet-
Stevens

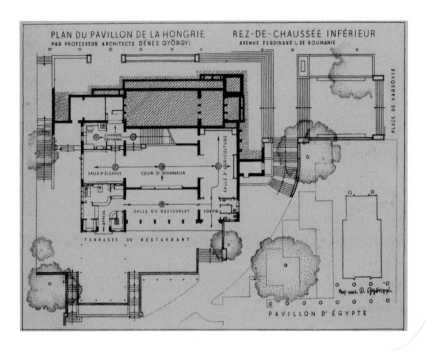

Le Ruban Bleu, monu-
mental entrance to the
exhibition on the quai
d'Orsay, architects
Debat-Ponsan, Fildier,
Sebillotte, Mestre

Plan of the Hungarian
Pavilion, architect
Denis Györgyi

Exterior of the
Hungarian Pavilion

The left bank of the
Seine with, from left to
right, the pavilions of
Sweden (Lind, Sven and
Ivar), Czechoslovakia
(Kresker, Bolivka) and
the United States
(Wiener, Higgins, and
Levi)

The modern movement – its humanist ideals more in keeping with the exhibition theme "The Art and Practice of Modern Life" – was represented, if overwhelmed. Notable among the modern buildings were Alvar Aalto's Finnish Pavilion and Josep Lluis Sert and Josep Lacasa's Spanish Pavilion. In contrast to the other great powers, the United States Pavilion (by Wiener, Higgins, and Levi) was a colorful and friendly modern structure with a central glass tower overlooking the Seine.

The opposition of classicism and modernism, each refusing compromise, reflected the world's greater struggle between nationalism and internationalism, conservatism and progressiveness.

The Aviation Pavilion,
architects Audoul,
Hartwig, and Gerodias.
Watercolor by Geo Ham

The Egyptian Pavilion,
a mix of ancient and
art deco forms, archi-
tect Roger Lardat

Overview of the exhibi-
tion site with the
German, Italian, and
Hungarian pavilions
clearly visible. Drawing
by André Maire

Entrance to the exhibi-
tion site at the Porte de
l'Alma

New York World's Fair New York

The Trylon and
Perisphere, architects
Wallace K. Harrison
and Fouilhoux

Plan of the exhibition
site

Year **1939 (30 April – 31 October); 1940 (11 May – 27 October)** Location **Flushing Meadows, Queens (the Corona Dumps)** Surface area **1,200 acres** Attendance **44,932,978** Participating nations **33** Fair president **Grover Whalen** Chairman board of design **Stephen F. Voorhees** Novelties **Air conditioning, color film, nylon stockings, television** Themes **Building the World of Tomorrow; For Peace and Freedom**

The Chrysler Pavilion,
architect James Gamble
Rogers

The Glass Center with
its tower of glass
bricks, architects
Shreve, Lamb &
Harmon

The Gas Pavilion, archi-
tects Skidmore &
Owings, John Moss

The Chrysler Pavilion

In 1939 New York held its second world's fair, and did so with considerably more success than it had in its first attempt of 1853. That initial fair took place in New York's own version of the Crystal Palace – modeled after the London original – erected in Manhattan on the site of what is now Bryant Park. Despite a large number of exhibitors and over one million visitors, that fair resulted in heavy losses for the private shareholders who financed it. The debacle scared off potential investors for some eighty years. The 1939 fair would be the fifteenth world exhibition held in the United States, (the twentieth, counting thematic exhibitions). During the fair, San Francisco held a much smaller exhibition to commemorate the completion of the Golden Gate Bridge.

History The impetus for the exhibition stemmed from the success of Chicago's Century of Progress Exposition, which provided considerable financial relief and a boost in morale to Depression-era Chicago. Public response to the proposed New York exhibition was overwhelmingly positive, and a nonprofit organization was quickly formed with its base of operations in the recently completed Empire State Building. After some controversy, politico Grover Whalen eventually assumed the presidency of the fair corporation, and, along with Parks Commissioner Robert Moses, took control of the event.

The year 1939, the 150th anniversary of the inauguration of George Washington as president of the United States, was chosen as the target date. But as the exhibition celebrated American democracy, Germany annexed Poland and a new war seemed inevitable. Poland was in fact represented at the exhibition, as were future Axis powers Italy and Japan. Germany had its own visions for the "World of Tomorrow" and did not participate.

Like it's New York predecessor, the 1939 world's fair ran a deficit. To make up for losses incurred during its first year of operation the fair corporation decided to hold the exhibition again in 1940. This time, however, its nature was radically changed. When the fair reopened on 11 May 1940, the Soviet Pavilion – which had drawn large crowds and had cost four million dollars to produce – was absent, demolished after Hitler and Stalin signed their infamous

The Marine Pavilion,
architects E. J. Kahn &
Muschenheim &
Brounn

The Bridge of Tomorrow,
architects Michael
L. Radoslovich and
Arthur Barzagli of the
Fair Corporation Design
Board

Constitution Avenue,
with the Trylon and
Perisphere in the back-
ground

Interior of the French
Pavilion, architects
Expert et Patout

nonaggression pact (the Japanese Pavilion, which was intended as a permanent structure, was arsoned after Pearl Harbor). The flags of the French and Polish pavilions were flown at half mast, and there was a general shift in accent from national boosterism to superficial amusement. Even this could not stem mounting losses. Nevertheless, another exhibition would be held on the same site in 1964, and again it would lose money.

Site   The 1939 fair was held on the former site of the Corona Dumps, an immense garbage heap in northern Queens famously described as "a valley of ashes" in F. Scott Fitzgerald's *The Great Gatsby*. Leveling the fill and creating an inhabitable – let alone inviting – home for an international exhibition was the first great challenge confronting the fair corporation, a challenge they met with great success. Today, the site is occupied by a massive city park, Flushing Meadows-Corona Park, upon which several structures remain from both the 1939 and 1964 exhibitions.

The fair site was divided into seven zones – amusement, communications, community interests, food, government, production and distribution, and transportation – each with a main exhibition hall. Broad, radial avenues separated the sectors. A central thoroughfare, Constitution Mall, ran between the still extant New York City Building (by Aymar Embury II) and the United States Building (by Howard L. Cheney). With the Manhattan skyline in the distance, the fair's buildings were kept low with a variety of vertical structures added as accent marks. The most striking of these were the blindingly white, 700-foot tall Trylon (triangular pylon) and its companion, the spherical Perisphere.

A concentrically planned color scheme gave order to the site. Painted avenues moved from the heart of the fair to its periphery in progressively deepening shades. The fair's carefully constructed order, however, quickly degenerated under the pressure of exhibitors who would not keep to their assigned spaces and a veritable avalanche of advertising and promotional paraphernalia.

The Soviet Pavilion, architects Boris Iofan and Karo S. Alabean

The Trylon and Perisphere from the Empire State Bridge. On the right is the dome of the United States Steel Pavilion by architects York & Sawyer with the assistance of the industrial designers Walter Dorwin Teague and G. F. Harrel

Architecture

The work produced under the direction of the fair's board of design – the body responsible for design regulations and their implementation – reflected the national outlook: conservatively modern. Large, blank wall surfaces were typical: windows took up valuable exhibition space, and air-conditioning made them unnecessary. The plaster wall surfaces provided ample room for paintings and reliefs executed in a moderne style. Alexander Calder and Isamu Noguchi, amongst others, provided sculptures.

The 1939 fair will always be best remembered for its Theme Center, comprised of Harrison and Fouilhoux's Trylon and Perisphere. These precise, geometric forms were connected by a 900-foot, elevated ramp – the Helicline – that offered fairgoers panoramic views of the site. Futuristic fantasy played a significant role in the popular exhibits of the fair, nowhere more so than in the Perisphere, which enclosed Democracity, a diorama of the "city of the future" designed by Henry Dreyfuss. Similar was Norman Bel Geddes Futurama – depicting a city in 1960 – which appeared in Albert Kahn's General Motors Pavilion (Kahn also designed the Ford Building). The most popular exhibit at the fair, it drew upwards of twenty-five million visitors.

The streamlining movement came to fore at the exhibition, most notably in the work of such industrial designers as Dreyfuss, Bel Geddes, Raymond Loewy, and Walter Dorwin Teague. Their sleek designs for everything from electric shavers to ocean liners were expressions of the ever-increasing velocity of modern life.

Vanguard modernism appeared in the undulating forms of Alvar Aalto's Finnish Exhibit (in the Hall of Nations); Oscar Niemeyer, Lucio Costa, and Paul Lester Weiner's free-form building for Brazil; Sven Markelius's elegant and widely-praised Swedish Pavilion; and the Swiss and Aviation pavilions by pioneer American modernist William Lescaze.

Plaza of Light seen from the General Electric Pavilion

One of the fair's most bizarre structures was surely Salvador Dali's Dream of Venus installation, a surreal cave-like pavilion with imitation coral plasterwork and erotic oceanic imagery. Inside, iconic Dali works were displayed alongside a tank with female bathers milking a bandaged cow.

Exposition Universelle et Internationale de Bruxelles (Expo '58) Brussels

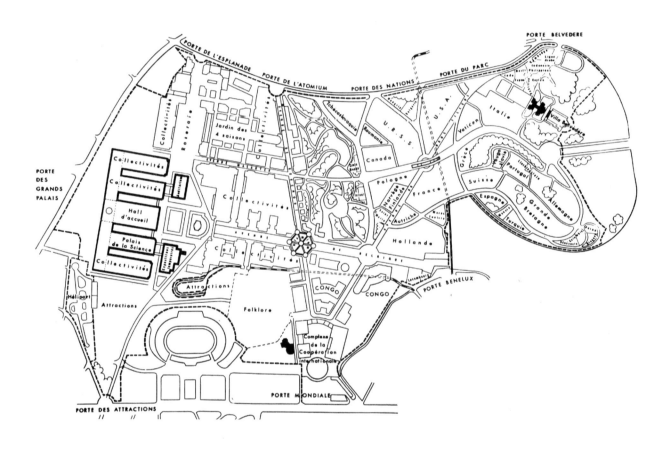

The Atomium

Plan of the exhibition site

Year **1958 (17 April – 19 October)** Location **Brussels (Heizelplateau)** Surface area **494 acres** Attendance **41.1 million** Participating nations **44** Chief Architect **J. Van Goethem** Novelty **Sputnik** Theme **Building the World on a Human Scale**

Of all the great exhibitions, the Exposition Universelle of 1958 is one of the least appreciated. Even in the host nation, Belgium, criticism was harsh. Many Belgians considered the fair's architecture to be overblown and artificial, and therefore in direct opposition of the exhibition's avowed theme of "Building the World on a Human Scale." As a result, Le Corbusier's swooping Philips Pavilion was mercilessly destroyed after the exhibition closed. In fact, the "inhuman" scale of the exhibition and its installations was in part the result of the exclusion of architects and planners from the planning process.

The site   The exhibition site overlapped that of the 1935 Brussels exhibition on the Heizelplateau, but was extended by as much again to create a far larger site. The Atomium, a 360-foot, aluminum-coated steel molecule formed the pivotal point between the Belgian section and the various foreign pavilions and served as the defining symbol of the fair. The Atomium was situated in a cramped, geometrically defined space, the pavilions in a landscaped setting. Additional space was set aside on the site's periphery for international organizations, including the European Community for Coal and Steel (forerunner of the EEC) and the United Nations. Popular entertainment, the Lunapark amusement zone, and the picturesque village of Old Belgium were located on the west side of the plot.

A critical appraisal   With the 1950s came the dawning realization that scientific progress was not always a blessing. This concern was reflected in the theme of the exhibition and in the brief to the participants, which stated that installations should honor "humankind in the fullest and most elevating sense of the word." The theme offered a marked contrast to the everyday reality of 1950s Brussels, a city convulsed by construction and development. For Belgians, the exhibition did not act simply as a metaphor for modernization, it played a part in the transformation of Belgium in general and Brussels in particular. For instance, space was cleared to provide parking facilities for no fewer than forty-five thousand cars. While the fair's Old Belgium installation proudly displayed art nouveau architecture, the real thing was being demolished at a rapid pace. In this context, the overwhelmingly negative Belgian reaction to the fair is understandable.

The Finnish Pavilion, architect Reima Pietilä

The Spanish Pavilion, architects Ramon Vazquez Molezun and José Antonio Corales

The English Pavilion,
architects H. V. Lobb
and J. C. Ratcliffe

Interior of one of the
Atomium's twenty hol-
low tubes. André
Waterkeyn, engineer

The Soviet Pavilion,
architects Y. Abramov,
A. Boretski, V. Doubov
and A. Polanski

The French Pavilion,
architect Guillaume
Gillet, engineers René
Sarger and Jean Prouvé

The Civil Engineering
Pavilion, architect Van
Doorselaere with the
assistance of Paduart
(an engineer)

Interior of the Civil
Engineering Pavilion

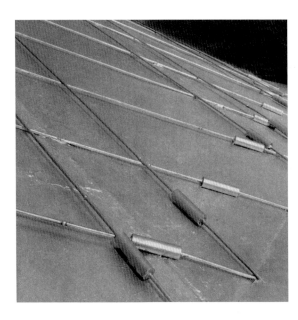

The Philips Pavilion,
architect Le Corbusier

Detail of the Philips
Pavilion construction
system of cables and
concrete slabs

The Norwegian
Pavilion with Plexiglas
corner columns, archi-
tect Sverre Fehn

Interior of the Japanese
Pavilion, architect
Kunio Mayekawa

The Atomium Like the Eiffel Tower, the Atomium created an uproar upon its completion, with detractors attacking it as a symbol of megalomaniacal bombast: "Human proportions and needs were sacrificed....The absurd costs and technical acrobatics of the 'Atomium' will only vanish from memory when this architectural monster is demolished" wrote one critic.[1]

The Atomium (engineer André Waterkeyn) was the exhibition's undoubted focal point, a molecule magnified 150 billion times. In stark contrast to the Sputnik satellite on view at the Soviet pavilion, it was intended as a symbol of peace in the midst of the Cold War. Containing both a restaurant and a bar, the construction stood on three legs, had nine spheres, and contained two staircases and an elevator. This "architectural monster," now in dire need of a facelift, was one of the few buildings to survive the exhibition, and – for better or worse – remains an enduring symbol of modern Brussels.

Architecture Several structurally flamboyant pavilions appeared at the fair. The best known of these remains Le Corbusier's "hyperbolic-parabaloid" pavilion for the Philips Company. Le Corbusier constructed this dynamic pavilion by mounting a series of individually molded small concrete slabs to a network of supporting cables. On the interior, an installation combined music, poetry, imagery, and a colorful light show in a synthetic production that the architect described as an "Electronic Game." The French Pavilion, by architect Guillaume Gillet with engineers René Sarger and Jean Prouvé, was also a demonstration of expressive angular form, a double-winged space frame with a giant cantilevered arm extending over the entrance. Similarly, the Civil Engineering Pavilion by Van Doorselaere with Paduart featured an immense cantilevered arm and an open interior space.

As always, the Soviet Pavilion was giant and bombastic, with a colossal statue of Lenin at its center. Conversely, the United States Pavilion – though also large – was intended as a statement of the openness of democracy and aimed to present an engaging demonstration of the American lifestyle. Other nations exhibited in various interpretations of the modern aesthetic, from the corporate internationalism of the German Pavilion by Egon Eiermann, Sep Ruf, and Rossow, to the Scandinavian cool of Sverre Fehn's Norwegian Pavilion, to the free-form play of Sergio Bernardes's Brazilian Pavilion.

The German Pavilion, architects Egon Eiermann, Sep Ruf, and Rossow, detail

The German Pavilion

1 Bonkelbal, p.51

Exhibition guide featuring the Atomium

The Dutch Pavilion, architects Van den Broek & Bakema, Gerrit Rietveld, Boks and Peutz

Century 21 Exposition Seattle

The Space Needle, architect John Graham

An artist's futuristic rendering of the fair's monorail system

Year **1962 (21 April – 21 October)** Location **Seattle** Surface area **74 acres** Attendance **9,609,609** Participating nations **24** Chairman, fair commission **Edward E. Carlson** Head of State **John F. Kennedy** Novelties **The Bubbleator, the *Friendship* 7 space capsule** Theme **Man's Life in the Space Age**

At the Brussels exhibition of 1958, the United States Pavilion presented a fashion show as its centerpiece while the rival Soviet Pavilion featured the Sputnik satellite. Before a European audience, American representation was intentionally focused on its democratic values and culture of freedom. But as the so-called space race accelerated, many Americans, including President John F. Kennedy, felt the nation was compelled to demonstrate its technological prowess, both to its own population and to the world at large. Seattle's Century 21 Exposition, with its science and space-oriented exhibits and its theme of "Man's Life in the Space Age," served this goal. NASA had its own pavilion (with astronaut John Glenn's *Friendship* 7 space capsule on display), and the official U.S. installation was devoted to science. Kennedy himself opened the exhibition – albeit remotely – using a telegraph key while on vacation in Florida.

Background
Initial planning for the event began with far more modest aspirations during a 1955 luncheon attended by many of Seattle's leading citizens (the original theme was to be "Festival of the West"). Edward E. Carlson, an energetic and well-connected hotel industry executive, was chosen as the chairman of the fair commission.

Seattle was fortunate to receive BIE blessing for the exhibition. In fact, the city's initial attempts to secure the organization's support were rebuffed: BIE was not favorably disposed to American petitions because the United States was not a BIE signatory; members of BIE thought Seattle too provincial a city; and New York and Moscow were also competing for the right to hold exhibitions. The Seattle commission pressed its case, however, and when BIE was foolishly belittled in the press by Robert Moses, the force behind the New York fair, BIE threw its support to Seattle.

The Space Needle's revolving restaurant

Brochure for theme exhibit "Man's Life in the Space Age"

The Space Needle under construction

Thai Pavilion with Space Needle in the background

The site After much debate amongst commission members, a site surrounding Seattle's Civic Auditorium was chosen for the event. Though small in area, it was centrally located, had good access to transportation, and was on solid ground (an important factor that differentiated it from other potential sites). Proximity to the city center allowed many of the buildings to be designed as permanent structures, a factor that would offset costs over the long term. A Design Standards Advisory Board was established to oversee site planning and architecture. Unlike many previous fairs, the Century 21 Exposition was not planned according to Beaux-Arts principles, with grand avenues and symmetrically deployed buildings. Instead, the pavilions were loosely clustered around the site: commercial exhibits were adjacent to the United States Science Pavilion, international pavilions surrounded the Washington State Coliseum, amusements were on the "Gayway," and other entertainment buildings sat in the vicinity of the centrally located stadium. An elevated monorail system brought visitors to the site from downtown via a 1.2-mile track. Two rubber-tired trains carried 450 passengers each on a 90-second trip back and forth from city to fair.

The Space Needle The visual centerpiece of the exhibition was the Space Needle, a 600-foot observation tower with a 220-seat revolving restaurant in its saucer-shaped observation platform. The initial idea for a tower came from Carlson, who was impressed by Stuttgart's 400-foot Television Tower while on vacation there (he was picking up a new Mercedes-Benz). Carlson thought a similar structure would be an appropriate symbol of and attraction to the Seattle fair. So did John Graham, an architect who had independently initiated work on a tower for the city that would pay for itself with entry fees and revenues from a restaurant. Graham submitted a design, it was accepted, and his firm privately financed the building. Finding a place for the tower on the exhibition grounds proved difficult, however. Due to its private financing, the structure could not be placed on land condemned by the government (as was most of the fair grounds). It was only after extensive research proved that a small parcel of land (a former fire station) had not been condemned that construction could move ahead.

Washington State
Colliseum, architect
Paul Thiry

United States Science
Pavilion, architect
Minoru Yamasaki

Pavilions The most striking of the pavilions was Paul Thiry's Washington State Coliseum, which has served as a civic arena since the exhibition shut its gates. Eleven stories tall and covering 4 acres, the building's most distinctive features are its expressionistic concrete buttresses and overhanging square roof. On the interior was the exhibition's theme exhibit, the "World of Tomorrow," designed by Donald Deskey. The exhibit began with one-hundred fairgoers riding a spherical elevator, the "Bubbleator, " to an elevated platform. There, they progressed through eight installations (including "Man's Past Futures," "Century 21 City," and "Your Future Today") before leaving at the "Exit to Now."

The United States Science Pavilion, actually a horseshoe of six linked buildings of varying heights, featured the fruits of American scientific research and was by far the most popular pavilion at the fair. Designed by Minoru Yamasaki, the concrete buildings were set on a plinth and separated from the other pavilions by a plaza with five aluminum Gothic towers. A film by Charles Eames stressed the relation of scientific progress to everyday life; Boeing's "Spacearium" took visitors on a simulated trip through outer space at the speed of light.

The Century 21 Exposition opened on schedule and closed with a tidy profit. An overflow of patrons attested to its success and popularity, and even led Bob Hope to quip that if there were a Century 21 doll, you would have to wind it up and then watch it stand on line.

New York World's Fair New York

Map of the exhibition with pavilions depicted in three-dimensions

Plan of the site divided into four zones

Year **1964 (22 April – 18 October); 1965 (21 April – 17 October)** Location **Flushing Meadows** Surface area **650 acres** Attendance **51,607,307 (27 million in 1964)** Participating nations **24** Fair president **Robert Moses** Novelty **The Ford Mustang, Belgian Waffles** Theme **Peace through Understanding**

Twenty-five years after the 1939 fair, Flushing Meadows was again the host of a large-scale event. Though it would ostensibly mark the tricentennial of New York, Robert Moses, the all-powerful city building commissioner and president of the World's Fair Corporation, had other motives. His intention was to use funds generated by the exhibition to create a massive city park on the site after the fair closed, a monument for posterity in his own name (the site had been left bare following the 1939 exhibition). Trouble loomed early when the ever-imperious Moses refused to even entertain BIE rules regarding the duration of the fair and the rents that could be imposed on exhibitors. Though BIE had often granted exemptions in the past, Moses' arrogant dismissal of BIE authority led the organization to actually request that its members not participate in the event. And most didn't, leaving a world exhibition without much of the world.

If an absence of foreign delegations was a major disappointment, the fair's gross mismanagement was ruinous. Moses – famed for his organizational acumen – planted the fair's administration with political hacks and cronies, none with prior experience in putting together a major exhibition; valuable contracts were awarded to friends and supporters with little accountability. In the end, the fair that Moses hoped would bankroll a new park became an unmitigated financial disaster.

Notwithstanding its problems, the fair did make a lasting mark on Flushing Meadows. The futuristic watchtowers of the New York State Pavilion are still extant (and were featured prominently in the recent film *Men in Black*). The exhibition's centerpiece, the giant steel globe known as the Unisphere, has also figured prominently as a setting for film makers, advertisers, and fashion photographers. And Flushing Meadows has been transformed into a heavily-used public park, the second largest in the city.

World Exhibitions

The watchtowers of the New York State Pavilion, architects Philip Johnson and Richard Foster. The tallest soars 226 feet

Official souvenir book featuring the Unisphere

OFFICIAL SOUVENIR BOOK OF THE NEW YORK

World's Fair

1965

IN BEAUTIFUL NATURAL COLOR $1.00

The site   The 1964 fair retained the plan and infrastructure of the 1939 exhibition – only the pavilions were positioned differently, this time arranged in thematic bands. In this sense, the plan resembled the design by Frédéric Le Play for the Paris exhibition of 1867. In fact, the fair's five person design committee – Wallace K. Harrison, Edward Durell Stone, Gordon Bunshaft, Henry Dreyfuss, and Emil Praeger – had wanted to house all of the exhibits in one gigantic building with sections leased to the various exhibitors: a reincarnation of the 1867 Main Building. Moses rejected this plan (it would not have generated enough rental fees). Instead, the far side of the Grand Central Parkway, a highway that cut across the site, was reserved for transportation pavilions; the areas adjacent to the Unisphere were assigned to the few foreign delegations that did appear and to the federal government and the American states; and a fourth zone was designated for industry. There was also a separate area for amusements, centered around Fountain Lake.

The Unisphere   The great symbol of the 1964 fair was the Unisphere. Sponsored by U.S. Steel, the twelve-story, stainless steel framework depicted the Earth with the continents in relief. The structure was designed by Peter Muller-Munk Associates, with landscaping by Gilmore Clarke. The immense globe stood on the same foundations that had supported a previous giant sphere: the Perisphere of 1939.

Unusual roofs   The aforementioned watchtowers formed part of the New York State Complex, which actually consisted of three towers, a theater, and the pavilion itself, better known as the Tent of Tomorrow. The pavilion had a giant ovular roof suspended from sixteen hollow, concrete columns, and was designed by the architects Philip Johnson and Richard Foster, assisted by the engineer Lev Zetlin. The flat roof, originally covered with colored plastic sheeting, was a double-diaphragm of steel cables. The 115-foot tall columns were cast on site and remain standing today. The exhibition space was on the ground level, providing a spectacular view upward. The pavilion featured work by contemporary Pop artists including Roy Lichtenstein, James Rosenquist, and Andy Warhol.

Two views of the
Unisphere, architect
Peter Muller-Munk
Associates, with the
*Fountain of the
Continents*, designed by
Gilmore Clark

221 New York 1964

The roof of the New York Port Authority Building was also unique: it doubled as a helipad. Designed by A. Gordon Lorimer, Ray Monte, E. Donald Mills and John Pile, the concrete building formed the shape of a giant T to stand for Transportation.

The Bell System exhibit, designed by Harrison & Abramovitz with Henry Dreyfuss as design consultant and Paul Weidlinger as structural engineer, was yet another structure in which the roof did more than just keep out the elements. Here, the domed exhibition structure collapsed the distinction between wall and ceiling.

Other pavilions
Glass, concrete, and steel dominated the exhibition. The IBM Pavilion, designed by Eero Saarinen just before his death, was an immense oval theater supported by a forest of steel trees, the foliage of which consisted of fourteen thousand gray-green panels. The building was intended to weather; its deliberately calculated corrosion would give the whole a natural appearance. The interior was by Charles Eames.

The glass Gas Pavilion, designed by Walter Dorwin Teague Associates, was located under two giant concrete slabs, the ribs of which terminated at a single, central pillar. The concrete Travelers Insurance installation by Kahn & Jacobs and Donald Deskey depicted two umbrellas (one upright, one inverted) interlocked to form a flying-saucer shape (the umbrella remains the company's logo to this day). Alaska's concrete pavilion was inspired by the igloo, and New Jersey's consisted of awnings artistically suspended from enormous masts.

The fair's attractions included Futurama II, a revised edition of the General Motors installation that had been so successful in 1939. This time it looked ahead to 2064. The fair also featured four installations designed by Walt Disney: the Ford, General Electric, Illinois, and Pepsi-Cola exhibits.

As it did for the 1939 fair, the city provided additional infrastructure for the fair, the most visible remnant being Shea stadium, home of the New York Mets. Perhaps the most enduring legacy of the fair has been the Panorama of the City of New York, a giant scale-model of the city housed in the New York City Pavilion. At a scale of 1 inch to 100 feet, it replicated nearly every building in the five boroughs of New York. Periodically updated, the panorama continues to draw crowds and is the centerpiece of the Queens Museum of Art, the occupant of the New York City Building since 1972.

The New York State Pavilion with its suspended roof, architects Philip Johnson and Richard Foster

The T-shaped Port Authority Building, architects A. Gordon Lorimer, Ray Monte, E. Donald Mills, and John Pile

United States Pavilion, architect Charles Luckman

The Bell Telephone Pavilion. Design by Harrison & Abramovitz, Henry Dreyfuss (design consultant) and Paul Weidlinger (structural engineer)

Tower of Light by Synergetics, Inc. and Robinson-Capsis-Stern Associates. The tower comprised 600 aluminum prisms from which shone the world's largest searchlights

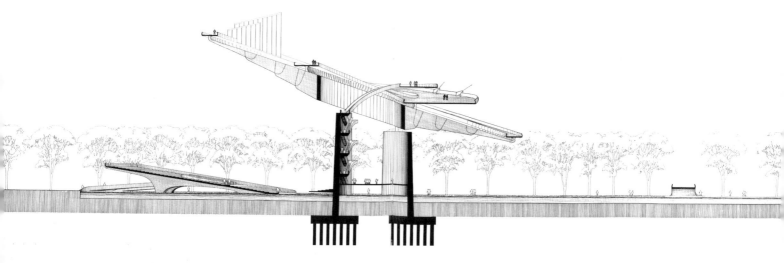

The Galaxon, designed by Paul Rudolph for the Portland Cement Company, was originally intended as the focal point of the exhibition, but the project was rejected

The Rocket Thrower by Donald Delue

The Austrian Pavilion, one of the few constructions in which wood was an inportant building material, architect Gustav Peichl

Enjoying the fair

The suspended Johnson Wax Theater, designed by Lippincott & Margulies in collaboration with Severud-Elstad-Krueger

FOUNTAINS OF THE FAIR

The fountains of the Unisphere in evening light

The Rotunda of the domeless Ford Pavilion architects, Welton Becket Associates
Designer: WED Enterprises, inc.
Construction: Thomas-Starrett Construction Company

Universal and International Exhibition
(Expo'67) Montreal

Interior of the U.S.
Pavilion, a geodesic
dome, architect
R. Buckminster Fuller

The Soviet Pavilion,
architect Michael
Vasilyevich Posokhin

Year **1967 (21 April – 27 October)** Location **Montreal (Cité du Havre, Île Sainte-Hélène, Île Notre-Dame)** Surface area **900 acres** Attendance **50,306,648** Participating nations **60** Commissioner General **Pierre Dupuy** Chief architect **Edouard Fiset** Theme **Man and His World**

After two earlier attempts to host an exhibition on the Île Sainte-Hélène, both thwarted by war, Montreal was finally successful on its third try. The date was auspicious: the centenary of Canadian independence. In contrast to the New York 1964 event, a lack of organizational experience did not prevent Expo '67 from achieving success; the widely acclaimed exhibition became the second largest ever held. Its $73 million shortfall was in reality a pittance when considering that with that money Montreal bought a new metro system, a series of roads and bridges, slum clearance, and a variety of new hotels and theaters. Today, many of the foreign pavilions, the administration building, and the Habitat residential project remain from the exhibition.

As was often the case, the initiative for the event was taken by private individuals who, after thorough groundwork, managed to gain the support of the necessary governmental authorities. This did not dispel a general skepticism about the event, largely prompted by the financial failure of the previous New York exhibition. But by the end of the fair, all doubts as to the ability of the Canadian planners were eliminated.

Theme The theme of the exhibition, "Man and his World," built on the humanist goals of the 1958 Brussels event. In the countercultural atmosphere of the late sixties, while war raged in Vietnam and Soviets and Americans faced off in the space race, the fair's administrators made a deliberate point that their event would not be a showcase for what they described as "cold" technology. Neither were they interested in creating a simple a amusement park.

World's Fairs

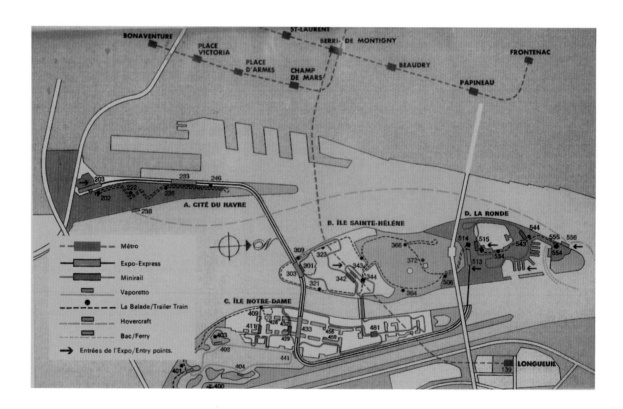

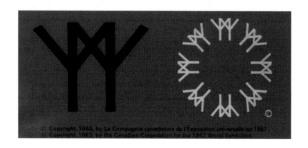

Habitat, architect
Moshe Safdie

Though not every nation kept to the theme – borrowed from the book *Terre des Hommes* by Antoine de Saint-Exupéry – the human scale was taken as a starting point by almost all of the exhibitors. Expo's logo, designed by Julien Hébert, consisted of stylized couples with outstretched and entwined hands suggesting love and friendship. The circle formed by the couples symbolized the world. One of the new bridges to the Île Sainte-Hélène was named Concordia (union).

Site In addition to the Concordia Bridge, designed by architect Claude Beaulieu, a second bridge, the Bridge of the Isles, was built across the St. Lawrence River. This was essential, as the exhibition was spread out across île Sainte-Hélène, the newly constructed Île Notre-Dame and the peninsula of the Cité du Havre. Thus, Montreal was the first to host a world exhibition on several islands, accessible via bridge and metro. On the site itself, visitors were transported by

The Czechoslovakian
Pavilion, architects
Miroslav Repa and
Vladimir Pycha

The U.S. Pavilion

Aerial view of the site

monorail. The pavilions were arranged in four clusters with water or greenery in between. Outdoor furniture and signage was designed for the exhibition by Paul Arthur Associates, and public areas were decorated with sculptures by Max Bill, Alexander Calder, and Jean Tinguely.

Habitat Prefabricated and modular construction had long been associated with modernism's humanist ideology and was thus eminently suited to the Expo '67 theme. Moshe Safdie, a young Israeli-born architect, exploited this association in his Habitat residential project, one of several thematic exhibitions at the fair. For Habitat, Safdie asymmetrically stacked a series of concrete modules, each roughly measuring 41 × 19 × 10.5 feet, to create twenty entirely unique apartments. These were then composed into an overall complex of 158 apartments accommodating seven hun-

Sculpture by Max Bill

dred residents: a remarkable achievement in differentiation through standardization. Habitat's cubic forms at once recall the blocky, stone architecture of Safdie's Israeli homeland and the geometry of European modernism. The complex has proven highly successful, now past its thirtieth year of continuous habitation.

The United States Pavilion   Like Habitat, the United States Pavilion carried strong – if highly sub-jective – ideological associations. The architect was R. Buckminster Fuller, "Bucky," the legendary guru and inventor of the geodesic dome, of which the U.S. Pavilion was the world's largest example. Fuller had spent a lifetime extolling the virtues of peace and the improvement of man's lot through technology and a scientific understanding of nature. Geodesic domes were his great success, appealing to virtually every segment of American society: members of the coun-terculture extolled them as holistic symbols of nature; the technically-minded admired their balance of forces; architects and artists applauded their elegance of form; military and corporate clients favored them for their low cost, stability, and easy fabrication; and the general public was seduced by Fuller himself. Seemingly offering something for everyone, Fuller's 250 foot-tall dome, actually a three-quarter sphere, became the defining symbol of the fair. Fuller was awarded the AIA Gold Medal for the building, which tragically burned during renovation in 1976. Today, its scorched framework still stands on the exhibition grounds.

Other Buildings If the U.S. Pavilion was both huge and ideologically appropriate, the Soviet Pavilion was simply huge. It's immense sloping roof rested on two enormous V-supports and was clearly visible through a glass curtain wall. The pavilion, designed by M. V. Posokhin, drew thirteen million visitors and was Expo's biggest attraction. Another mechanical marvel was Frei Otto and Rolf Gutbrod's German Pavilion, which made use of a cable construction system. The Dutch Pavilion by architects Eijkelenboom and Middelhoek was also an elaborate space-frame structure.

Inspired by the Montreal exhibition, the architects of Osaka 1970 would create even more fantastic pavilions of technological daring, creativity, and playfulness.

The Swiss Pavilion,
architect Werner
Gantenbein

Transportation by
Monorail

The German Pavilion,
architects Frei Otto and
Rolf Gutbrod

The scuplture
L'Homme/Man by
Alexander Calder

Japan World Exhibition (Expo '70) Osaka

The Takara Beautilion Pavilion, architect Kisho Kurokawa

The Fuji Group Pavilion, architect Yutaka Murata

Year **1970 (15 March – 13 September)** Location **Osaka (Senri Hills)** Surface area **865 acres** Attendance **64.2 million** Participating nations **38** Chief architect **Kenzo Tange** Novelties **Inflatable buildings, music composed by computer** Theme **Progress and Harmony for Mankind**

Japan had made repeated attempts to host a world's fair, but, for a variety of reasons, had failed to achieve that goal. So in 1965, when the Bureau Internationale des Expositions awarded Osaka a universal exhibition, the first ever to be held in Asia, the country was determined to triumph. The fair's planning committee originally intended that all of the installations would be placed under one roof, a megastructure in the spirit of the 1851 world exhibition. But, as it had been at the New York fair of 1964, this goal was quickly abandoned, largely under pressure from corporate sponsors who did not wish to cede their individual identities by being cast under one all-encompassing roof. The established tradition of individual pavilions would remain.

Criticism Expo '70 was not well received by Western architectural critics. Many felt that not deviating from the established formula of separate pavilions was a cop out, that there was little room for whimsy, and that, with no coordinated color scheme, the fair had a dull, concrete-gray appearance. The first two of these objections were unjustified; the third ignored the postwar Japanese tradition of building in *beton brut,* a tradition inspired by Le Corbusier. The idea for an all-encompassing structure had stemmed from Expo '67, where several buildings – most notably Fuller's U.S. Pavilion – were actually large superstructures with smaller installations contained inside. At Osaka, this trend did in fact continue with Kenzo Tange's gigantic Symbol Zone, which contained the Expo Museum of Fine Arts, Festival Plaza, the Symbol Area, the Theme Pavilion, and the colossal three-faced sculpture *Tower of the Sun.* The international and commercial pavilions – all different and all deliberately designed to be as conspicuous as possible – sat on either side of the Symbol Zone. Today, appreciation for the heterogeneous architecture of the Osaka 1970 exhibition has deservedly increased.

Plan of the exhibition site

EQUIPMENTAL ROAD
PAVILION
PARKING
GREENS
RECREATION ZONE

The Symbol Zone, a
giant space-frame struc-
ture designed by archi-
tect Kenzo Tange

Site and planning Criticism of an entirely different order was voiced over the fact that "Progress," the much-lauded theme of the exhibition, had been hard on the Japanese environment. The country's teeming cities were unplanned, unsanitary, and disorderly. Narrow streets could not cope with modern traffic, and precious little money was expended on the design of public space. Architects had been up in arms over these conditions since the early 1960s, but their protestations were largely unheeded. Among the generation of architects disturbed by what they saw around them were the Metabolists, a group founded in 1960 by leading young architects including Kiyonori Kikutake and Kisho Kurokawa. Like the British group Archigram, the Metabolists envisioned the city as a megastructure of mobile, dispos-able dwellings constructed of modular parts. The Metabolists were a major presence at the fair, and the spirit of their work infused exhibition. Expo '70 provided tremendous incentive for infrastructural improvement to the host city. Osaka, Japan's second largest city after Tokyo, invested two billion dollars in the exhibition, and an additional eight billion was pumped into the city itself.

If the nineteenth century fairs called for a brotherhood of nations, Kenzo Tange, Expo '70's chief architect, sought a brotherhood of man, a forum where diverse people could come closer together. The Festival Plaza, situated at the center of the site in the Symbol Zone, was earmarked for just this purpose. The spatial organization of the event was similarly intended to express both harmony and diversity. Tange linked the immense Symbol Zone structure – which spanned a highway that divided the site – to smaller plazas using enclosed and air-conditioned moving sidewalks. Metaphorically, the Symbol Zone represented the trunk of a great tree; the sidewalks were its branches; the pavilions its colorful blooms. The foreign pavilions were placed to one side of the megastructure, the Japanese government installations and many of the commercial structures to the other. Landscaped gardens were provided for relaxation and amusement, and a mono-rail transported visitors around the site.

The Toshiba-IHI
Pavilion, architect Kisho
Kurokawa

The Swiss Pavilion,
architect Willi Walter

Bird's-eye view of the exhibition site

Cross-section of Symbol Zone with the protruding *Tower of the Sun*

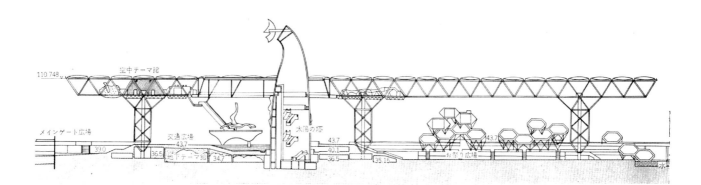

Architecture Of the many eye-catching structures of the exhibition, the Symbol Zone was the largest: a 354 x 1,000 foot megastructure with six legs for support and a 230-foot sculpture (Taro Okamoto's *Tower of the Sun*) piercing its space-frame roof. The outstretched arms of the sculpture welcomed visitors to the exhibition. Two smaller sculptures, *Motherhood* and *Youth*, symbolized growth, dignity, boundless energy, and the progress of the human race.

The Metabolists were represented by several architects: Kikutake was responsible for the remarkable 417-foot Expo Tower. Kurokawa's Takara Beautilion Pavilion – themed "The Joy of Being Beautiful" – had a framework of modular bent steel units, and his Toshiba-IHI Pavilion – housing a theater with nine screens – was built using a high-tension truss of 1,500 steel tetrahedrons. But the most extraordinary of all was Sachio Otani's Sumitomo Fairytale Pavilion, a series of nine space-frame towers supporting spherical display modules and a two-hundred seat auditorium.

Inflatable construction systems were also on display. The American Pavilion (by Davis, Brody, Chermayeff, Geismar, de Harak Associates) was actually a pit dug into the earth that was covered with a fiberglass canopy held in place by air-pressure and steel cables. The Fuji Group Pavilion, designed by Yukata Murata, consisted of sixteen immense "air beams" that were inflated and belted together to specifications that could withstand a typhoon. An inflatable roof also covered the space frame of Festival Plaza.

Other notable structures included the Australian Pavilion (by James MacCormick), which had a saucer-shaped 200-ton auditorium suspended from a towering cement "sky hook." Adjacent to the auditorium was the "Space Tube," an installation viewed while riding along moving platforms in an industrial-looking cylindrical structure. Willi Walter's Swiss Pavilion, the "Tree of Light," was comprised of a system of aluminum pipes and thirty-five thousand light bulbs that were illuminated at night. The French Pavilion, designed and fabricated by the Shimizu Construction Corporation, was a series of interlocked, white geodesic domes. A variety of additional pavilions – from foreign nations and commercial exhibitors – were similarly creative and visually arresting.

The U.S. Pavilion, architects Davis, Brody, Chermayeff, Geismar, and de Harak Associates

The Soviet Pavilion, architects Mosproject, M. V. Posokhin, A. N. Kondratjev, V. A. Svirski

The Dutch Pavilion, architect Jacob B. Bakema in collaboration with Carel Weeber

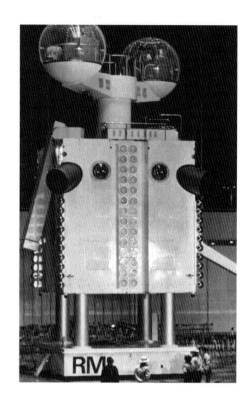

The French Pavilion,
architect Shimizu
Construction
Corporation

Giant Robot in Festival
Hall

The Gas Pavilion, archi-
tect Ohbayashi-Gumi
Ltd.

Aerial view of the
Australian Pavilion,
architect James
MacCormick, structural
engineer Norman Sneath

The Automobile Pavilion,
architect Kunio Maekawa

The Sumitomo Fairytale
Pavilion, architect
Sachio Otani

Universal Exposition Seville

The Finnish Pavilion,
architects Jääskeläinen,
Kaakko, Rouhiainen,
Sanaksenaho,
Tirkkonen

La Barqueta-Mapfre
bridge by Santiago
Calatrava. The exhibi-
tion site is on the right

Year **1992 (20 April – 12 October)** Location **Seville, La Cartuja Island** Surface area **415 acres** participating nations **108** Expo president **Jacinto Pellón** Theme **The Era of Discoveries**

After Osaka 1970, it was twenty-two years before another universal exhibition opened. The host was Seville, the second time in its history that the city had held such an event. The first time, in 1929, a smaller, theme exhibition stressed the historic link between the port and Spain's overseas colonies. The 1992 exhibition marked the five-hundredth anniversary of the discovery of the New World, and was thus a fitting sequel to the earlier event. It was originally intended that Chicago would commemorate Columbus's famous journey with a simultaneous exhibition, but having already hosted exhibitions in 1893 and 1933, Chicago canceled at the last moment.

Background   The initiative for the exhibition came in 1976 from the Spanish king, Juan Carlos, and was followed up by a more concrete proposal from Felipe Gónzalez, the Socialist prime minister and native of Seville. His aspirations for the event, however, exceeded a world exhibition to include much new infrastructure for the city: an airport, a train station, a high-speed railway to Madrid, highway construction. Under his direction, all manner of public works were carried out. For Gónzalez, the event signaled a new, international role for Seville. To help offset the costs for these improvements, Spain was also able to draw on European funding for disadvantaged areas, which meant that the Seville exposition was probably the first financed with foreign capital.

The site   La Cartuja, an artificial island in the Guadalquivir River, was chosen as the exhibition site. The island, named after the Carthusian convent Santa Maria de las Cuevas, was built as a measure to keep the Guadalquivir in check and to protect the city from flooding. Originally, the dry and arid area along the river lay fallow, but after extensive work was completed in 1975, Seville was left with a large area fit for development. The exhibition site covered but a small part of this area. The cultivating and planting of the site and the adjoining sports and recreation areas was a chore rivaled only by the clearing of Forest Park for the 1094 exhibition in St. Louis, and the leveling of the Corona Dumps for the 1939 New York fair.

One of the most important tasks the fair's designers had to grapple with was how to restore the relationship between the site and the historic city center, which was cut off from the river by an obsolete rail yard. A new promenade was

The Belgian Pavilion,
architects Driessen,
Meersman and Thomas

The Alamillo bridge by Santiago Calatrava. The exhibition site is on the left

designed along the waterfront and no fewer than six bridges were built over the river, doubling the existing number. A competition was held for the design of the site, but, as with the 1851 exhibition, the organizers thanked the entrants for their trouble and proceeded on an entirely different course. This was due in part to major changes to the program made after the competition brief was published. For instance, it was anticipated that sixty foreign nations would take part in the exhibition, but 108 signed up during the planning phase.

Regardless, the competition-winning design by Emilio Ambasz failed to link the site with the historic city. It did, however, allow the river to penetrate deep into the exhibition site, metaphorically flooding it with a series of small pools. The plan that was adopted similarly failed to bring about an interaction between old and new. The breadth of the river warranted bold structures that would look out across the city and provide visual interest from the promenade on the opposite bank. Instead, the fair offered a fragmented panorama with the pavilions facing away from the city, not toward it. Moreover, a highway along the river's edge created an unwelcome boundary line between city and exposition site.

The exhibition site, roughly divided into three zones, also lacked inspiration. The Spanish regional pavilions, with their backs to the city, formed a cramped semicircle around a large pool. The international pavilions were arrayed to the sides of five parallel avenues at right angles to a canal running through the site. Permanent buildings, including the Trian Tower (by Francisco J. Saénz de Oiza) and the Pavilion of Discoveries (by Javier Feduchi and Eduardo Arroyo), were placed in a third zone. To provide scenic landscaping and shade for the extremely hot site, the fair's architectural commission planted some thirty-two thousand trees.

Architecture Though the plan was unexceptional, the buildings constructed for the event reflected the sophistication of contemporary Spanish architecture. The new railway station and airport (by Cruz/Ortiz and Rafael Moneo, respectively), the restoration of La Cartuja (Francisco Torres), and the Trian Tower all exhibited intellectual clarity and visual grace.

The pavilions were characterized by an abundance of subdued colors (in contrast to the gray of Osaka), meticulous detailing, and expensive and specially manufactured materials. If concrete was the material of choice at Osaka, at Seville walls were of natural stone and easily assembled sheeting. Among the many noteworthy structures, Santiago Calatrava's Kuwaiti Pavilion, with its mechanical roof, stands out. At midday, to provide protection from the heat, the roof closed by means of large wooden "claws" that folded together. Calatrava was also responsible for two stunning bridges spanning the Guadalquivir. Tadao Ando's Japanese Pavilion was similarly impressive, offering an almost holy aura.

The Kuwaiti Pavilion, architect Santiago Calatrava

The Finnish Pavilion

Plan of the exhibition
site

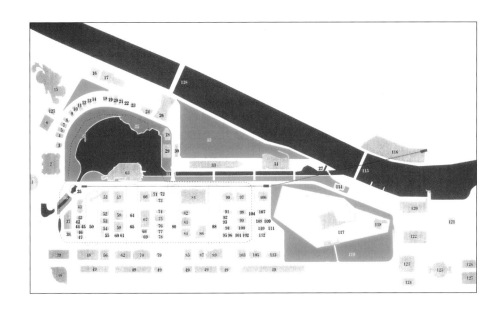

The French Pavilion,
architects Viguier, Jodry
and Seigneur

Interior of the Italian
Pavilion, architects Gae
Aulenti, Pierluigi
Spadolini.

World's Fairs

Emilio Ambasz's competition-winning proposal for the site

The Chilean Pavilion, architect José Cruz Ovalle

EXPO2000
HANNOVER

The World Exposition

Expo 2000 Hanover

The Expo 2000 logo, designed by Iris Utikal and Michael Gais from the Qwer group, is the result of a competition

The Expo 2000 mascot, designed by Javier Mariscal, designer of the mascot for the 1992 Olympics in Barcelona

Year **2000 (1 June – 13 October)** Location **Hanover, Kronsberg** surface area **400 acres** Attendance **40 million (estimated)** Participating nations **180 (estimated)** Theme **Man, Nature, Technology**

Hanover BIE has awarded the much anticipated millennial exhibition for the year 2000 to the city of Hanover. After 150 years and many important national and thematic exhibitions – such as the Deutscher Werkbund of 1914 and the Weissenhofseiedlung of 1927 – Germany has finally secured a world exhibition of the highest category. Whether the new millennium, technically speaking, begins in the year 2000 or 2001 will remain a controversial footnote in the exhibition's history.

The exhibition theme – "Mankind, Nature, Technology" – will be exhaustively expounded in a million square foot theme park, with subthemes of "Health and Nutrition," "Living and Working," "Milieu and Environment," "Communication and Information," "Recreation and Mobility," and "Education and Culture." The organizing committee is particularly interested in the relationship between the environment and technological progress. Following the exhibition, the theme park will be converted into the "International Academy of the Future," which will continue to address these issues. The Hanover exhibition will be universal in the true sense of the word: projects relating to the fair's theme from all over the world will be connected to the site via satellite. Virtual projects will put a new spin on the traditionally temporary architecture of exhibition buildings.

In keeping with the economic and environmental objectives of the event, an existing convention complex will serve as the central hall, something normally forbidden and for which special dispensation had to be first given by BIE. The master plan is by the Frankfurt firm Albert Speer & Partner, and includes not only the actual exhibition site, but the area in the immediate vicinity, a residential complex, and surrounding infrastructure. The firm von Gerkan, Marg and Partner will design the exhibition's theme park. With a variety of structural improvements, including a revamped rail system, Hanover is busily preparing itself for the event and the 300,000 visitors it expects to receive each day.

The Dutch pavilion with its environmentally friendly green layer and the energy-saving windmills. Design MVRDV

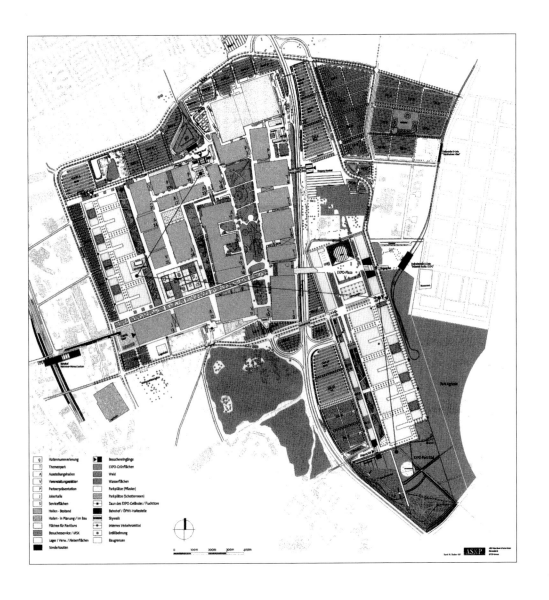

Master plan for Expo
2000 with the existing
convention hall in
orange and new
pavilions in yellow

Examples of the
possible arrangements
of foreign pavilions on
the specially assigned
plots

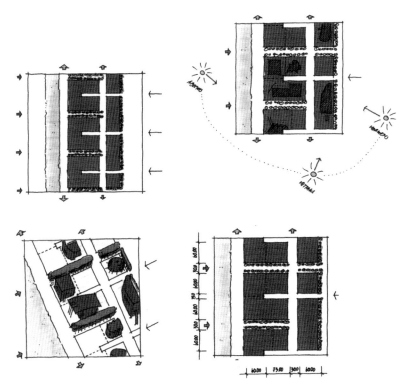

World's Fairs

General

Allwood, John, *The Great Exhibitions*, London 1977.

Beutler, Christian, *Weltausstellungen im 19. Jahrhundert*, Munich 1973.

Friebe, Wolfgang, *Buildings of the World Exhibitions*, Leipzig 1985.

K.V.G.O. (Koninklijk Verbond voor Grafische Ondernemers) *Kerstnummer Grafisch Nederland*, 'Wereldtentoonstellingen,' 1991.

Poirier, René, *Des foires, des peuples, des expositions*, Brussels 1958.

Le livre des expositions universelles 1851–1989, Paris 1983.

Specific

Album de l'Exposition 1900: 120 Vues et 7 Plans, Paris 1900.

"Arts et techniques dans la vie moderne," *Exposition Paris 1937* no. 4, August 1936.

Arts industriels et du métier, exposition universelle et internationale: Bruxelles 1910, Antwerp 1910.

Baalman, Dirk, "De wereldtentoonstelling van 1883 in Amsterdam," *Kunstlicht* 9, 1983, 5–11.

Barré-Despond, Arlette, and Suzanne Tise, *Jourdain*, New York 1991.

Bastlud, Knud, and Sigfried Giedion, *José Luis Sert*, Zurich 1967.

Benevolo, Leonardo, *History of Modern Architecture*, Cambridge (Mass.) 1977.

Bekaert, Geert, and Francis Strauven, *Bouwen in België 1945–1970*, Brussels 1971.

Berlage, H.P., *Beschouwingen over bouwkunst en hare ontwikkeling*, Rotterdam 1911.

Boesiger L., and H. Girsberger, eds., *Le Corbusier, 1910–65*, Zurich 1967.

Bontridder, Albert, "Dialoog tussen licht en stilte," in *Hedendaagse bouwkunst in België*, Antwerp 1963.

Boyce, Robert, *Keck & Keck*, New York 1993.

Brunhammer, Yvonne and Suzanne Tise, *Les Artistes Décorateurs 1900–1942*, Paris 1990.

Bruxelles et l'Exposition 1910, Antwerp 1910.

Caro, Robert A., *The Power Broker*, New York 1974.

Chemetov, Paul, and Bernard Marrey, *Architectures Paris 1848–1914*, Paris 1980.

Committee of the Second Architectural Convention of Japan, *Structure, Space, Mankind: Expo '70*, Osaka 1970.

Cordat, Charles, *La Tour Eiffel*, Paris 1955.

Corneli, R., *Antwerpen und die Weltausstellung*, 1886.

Cremona, Italo, *De wereld van de Jugendstil*, Amsterdam 1969.

The Crystal Palace Exhibition, Illustrated Catalogue: An Unabridged Republication of the Art Journal Special Issue, New York 1970.

Dean, David, *Architecture of the 1930s. Recalling the English Scene*, New York 1983.

De Long, David G., ed., *American Architecture: Innovation and Tradition*, New York 1986.

Deutschland's Raumkunst und Kunstgewerbe auf der Weltausstellung zu Brüssel, Stuttgart 1910.

Doctorow E. L., *World's Fair*, New York 1985.

Drexler, Arthur, ed., *The Architecture of the Ecole des Beaux-Arts*, London 1977.

"Expo 70," *Architectural Review*, CXLVIII, 882, 1970.

"Expo '70," *Deutsche Bauzeitung* 7, no. 104, July 1970.

Expo '92 Sevilla Pabellon de Belgica, Antwerp 1992.

Expo '92 Seville, Architecture and Design, Seville 1992.

"L'Exposition des Arts Décoratifs" *Art et Décoration*, July–December 1925.

Evenson, Norma, *Paris: A Century of Change 1878–1978*, New Haven 1979.

Ferreira de Almeida, *Exposiçoes Universais, Barcelona 1929*, Lisbon 1995.

Findling, John E., *Chicago's Great World's Fairs*, New York, 1994.

Fox, Timothy J., and Duane R. Sneddeker, *From the Palaces to the Pike*, St. Louis 1997.

Freeland, J. M., *Architecture in Australia, a History*, Melbourne 1968.

Garofalo, Francesco and Luca Veresani, *Adalberto Libera*, New York, 1992.

Gers, Paul, *En 1900*, 1900.

Gilliam, Harold, and Phil Palmer, *The Face of San Francisco*, New York 1960.

Gournay, Isabelle, *Le nouveau Trocadéro*, Liège 1985.

Gazette des Architectes et du Batiment, Paris 1865.

Gréber, Jacques, *L'Architecture aux Etats-Unis*, Paris 1920.

Harada, Jiro, The Panama-Pacific International Exposition and its Meaning, *The Studio* LXV, no. 269, August 1915.

Harris, Neil, et. al., *Grand Illusions: Chicago's World's Fair of 1893*, Chicago 1993.

L'Illustration, "Exposition Paris 1937," Paris 1937.

Jager, Ida, *Willem Kromhout*, Rotterdam 1992.

The Japan Architect 127, January–February 1970.

Kalff L. C., *Kunstlicht und Architektur*, Eindhoven 1943.

Kinchin, Perilla & Juliet, *Glasgow's Great Exhibitions*, Wendlebury 1988.

Klasen, Ludwig, *Grundriss-Vorbilder von Gebäuden für Kunst und Wissenschaft*, Leipzig 1887.

Klein, Dan, Nancy A. McClelland, and Malcolm Haslan, *Art Deco*, Alphen aan den Rijn 1995.

Kraemer, Hans, *Das XIX. Jahrhundert in Wort und Bild*, Berlin, n.d.

Kultermann, Udo, ed., *Kenzo Tange Architecture and Urban Design 1946–1969*, Zurich 1970.

Laville, Michel, "Expo 67 in Montreal" *Werk* 11, November 1967, 708–30.

Le Corbusier, *Het electronische Gedicht/Le Corbusier*, Eindhoven 1958.

Lenning, Henry F, *The Art Nouveau*, The Hague 1951.

Linn, James Weber, *The Official Pictures of a Century of Progress Exposition*, Chicago 1933.

Loyrette, Henri, *Gustave Eiffel. Ein Ingenieur und sein Werk*, Stuttgart 1985.

Maass, John, *The Glorious Enterprise*, New York, n.d.

Mendoza, Eduardo, *Stad der wonderen*, Amsterdam 1988.

Montreal Expo '67, De Mens in de Delta, de Nederlandse deelneming aan de Wereldtentoonstelling Montreal 1967, 1968.

Montijn, Ileen, *Kermis van koophandel, De Assterdamse wereldtentoonstelling van 1883*, Bussum 1983.

Monzie, Anatole De, *Pavilion Société des Artistes Décorateurs. Exposition Internationale Paris-1937*, Paris 1937.

Morgan, Murray, *Century 21*, Seattle 1963.

Newhall, Ruth, *San Francisco's Enchanted Palace*, Berkeley 1967.

Nicoletti, Manfredi, *D'Aronco e l'archittura liberty*, Rome 1982.

De Opmerker 18, 1883.

Orandakan, 's-Gravenhage 1970.

The Overseas Construction Association of Japan, *Japan's Construction 1970*, Tokyo n.d.

Panman, J., *Gids Wereldtentoonstelling Brussel '58*, Amsterdam 1958.

De Panoramische droom, Antwerpen en de wereldtentoonstellingen 1885, 1894, 1930, Antwerp 1993.

Le pavillon de la Hongrie a l'exposition internationale de Paris 1937, Budapest 1937.

Pevsner, Nikolaus, *History of Building Types*, London 1976.

Pevsner, Nikolaus, and J. M. Richards, eds., *The Anti-Rationalists*, London 1973.

Prims, Lut, and Ronny de Meyer, *Het Zuid: Antwerpen 1875-1890*, Antwerp 1993.

Quantrill, Malcolm, *Alvar Aalto, A Critical Study*, New York 1983.

Ragon, Michel, *Histoire mondiale de l'architecture et de l'urbanisme modernes*, 1971.

Roth, Leland M., *A Concise History of American Architecture*, New York 1980.

Roth, Leland M., McKim, *Mead & White, Architects*, London 1983.

Rydell, Robert W., *World of Fairs*, Chicago 1993.

Scharabi, M, *Architekturgeschichte des 19 Jahrhunderts*, Berlin 1993

Schulze, Franz, *Mies van der Rohe, Critical Essays*, New York 1989.

Selle, Gert, *Jugendstil und Kunstindustrie*, Darmstadt 1974.

Simon, Alfred, *Bundesrepublik Deutschland, Planen und Bauen*, Bonn 1973.

Sinkevitch, Alice, ed., *AIA Guide to Chicago*, San Diego 1993.

Speer, Albert, ed., *Neue Deutsche Baukunst*, Berlin 1941.

Stern, Robert A. M., Gregory Gilmartin, and Thomas Mellins, *New York 1930: Architecture and Urbanism between the Two World Wars*, New York 1987.

Stern, Robert A. M., Thomas Mellins, and David Fishman, New York 1960, *Architecture and Urbanism Between the Second World War and the Bicentennial*, New York 1995.

Teirlinck, Herman, *Brussel 1900*, Antwerp 1981.

Trachtenberg, Marvin, *The Statue of Liberty*, Middlesex 1974.

The Universal Exposition Beautifully Illustrated, St. Louis 1904.

Waldo, Myra, *Japan Expo '70 Guide*, New York 1970.

Walton, Ann Thorson, *Ferdinand Boberg, Architect: The Complete Work*, Cambridge (Mass.) 1994.

Wilde, Otto, and Albert Ganzlin, eds., *Weltausstellung Chicago*, Berlin 1893.

Willensky, Elliot and Norval White, *AIA Guide to New York City*, New York 1988.

Wilson, Edwin, *The Wishing Tree*, Sydney 1992.

Windsor, Alan, *Peter Behrens: Architect and Designer*, London 1981.

Witherspoon, Margaret Johanson, *Remembering the St. Louis World's Fair*, St. Louis 1973.

The WPA Guide to New York City, New York, 1939.

Index

Included in the index are the architects, engineers and designers cited in the text. Entries are followed by years of participation.

Colophon

Production co-ordination Cees de Jong, Emmanuelle Kramps, V+K Publishing, Blaricum

Author, illustration research Erik Mattie, Amsterdam

Design Cees de Jong, Jan Johan ter Poorten, Corine Teuben, V+K Design, Blaricum

Lithography Propress, Wageningen

Printing Emico Offset, Wommelgem

Translation Lynn George, Norfolk

Acknowledgements Antiquariaat Opbouw Amsterdam, Bart van den Berg, Coert Peter Krabbe, Gerrit Oorthuys, Jouke van der Werff Architectura & Natura Amsterdam, Deutsche Bahn A.G., Expo 2000 Hanover GmbH

Photo credits William Henry Fox Talbot, p.12 right; Missouri Historical Society, p.117, p.119, p.120; Kollar, p.184; *Domus*, p.203, p.207 top; Marc, p.205; *Architectural Design*, p.207 below; Persdienst (Press Service), p.209 below; DLR + John Graham Associates Architects/ Engineers/Planners, p.210, p.212, p.213 top and bottom left; Minoru Yamasaki Associates, p.215; Robert Perron, p.229; Leonardo Bezzola, p.231; *Deutsche Bauzeitung*, p.234, p.238; *Architectural Review*, p.237; Jouke van der Werff, p.244, p.248, p.250; Nederlandse Stichting voor Wereldtentoonstellingen, p.254 top.

Entries for St. Louis 1904, Chicago 1933, and Seattle 1962 have been provided by Princeton Architectural Press, New York

Every effort has been made to settle the publication rights and credit for the reproductions in this book. Any persons or organizations who have not been correctly credited with respect to the reproductions should contact to V+K Publishing, Blaricum